W9-CXP-052

ISO 9000....A Legal Perspective

by
James W. Kolka, PhD, JD

ISO 9000...A Legal Perspective

by

James W. Kolka, PhD, JD

co-published by

American Society for Quality

International Forum for Management Systems, Inc.

ISO 9000...A Legal Perspective
by James W. Kolka, PhD, JD

Co-Published by
International Forum for Management Systems, Inc. (INFORM)
15913 Edgewood Drive
Montclair, VA 22026

American Society for Quality (ASQ)
611 East Wisconsin Avenue
Milwaukee, WI 53202-4606

This publication is designed to provide accurate and authoritative information in regard to the subject matter covered. It is sold with the understanding that the publisher is not engaged in rendering legal, accounting or other professional services. If legal advice or other expert assistance is required, the services of a competent professional should be sought.

Library of Congress Cataloging-in-Publication Data
Kolka, James W.
    ISO 9000...A Legal Perspecitve / James W. Kolka
Library of Congress Catalog Card Number: 97-077604
ISBN: 1-891578-00-6

Printed in the United Stated of America

Publisher .... *James P. Gildersleeve*
Senior Editor .... *James G. Mroz*
Managing Editor .... *A. Kevin Baynes*
Production/Design .... *A. Kevin Baynes*
First Edition.

10 9 8 7 6 5 4 3 2 1

Table of Contents

Extended Table of Contents vi
About the Author x
About the Publishers xii
Acknowledgements xiv
Foreword xvi

Main Section:

Introduction 3

Scenario 1 5

Chapter I —
Introduction to ISO 9000 11

Scenario 2 25

Chapter II —
Legal Implications of an ISO 9001-based QMS 33

Scenario 3 47

Chapter III —
Quality Systems and Product Safety 55

Chapter IV —
Beyond ISO 9001/2/3...A Preventive Program 73

Chapter V —
ISO 9000 & the Harmonization of National Laws 97

Appendicies:

A   ISO 9001—An Overview of the Clauses
     ...and Their Meaning 119

B   EU Directive...The Product Liability Directive 137

C   EU Directive...The Product Safety Directive 149

D   Japanese Law...Guide to the Product Liability Law
     (Law No. 85, 1994) 169

E   Sources for More Information 179

Extended Table of Contents

Table of Contents v
Extended Table of Contents vi
About the Author x
About the Publishers xii
Acknowledgements xiv
Foreword xvi

Main Section:

Introduction 3
Scenario 1 5
   The Case 6
   The Attack and Defense 6
   Conclusions 8
   Other Considerations 9
Chapter I —
Introduction to ISO 9000 11
   Key Points 12
   The Origins of ISO 9000 13
   Elements of the ISO 9000 Series 13
      Table 1-1: The Structure of ISO 9004-1 Quality Management
            and Quality System Elements—Guidelines 15
      Table 1-2: The 20 Clauses and Subclauses of ISO 9001,
            Section 4, Quality System Requirements 17
      Table 1-3: The ISO 9000 Guidance Standards 19
   Why Companies Register 20
   Summary 22
Scenario 2 25
   The Case 26
   The Attack and Defense 26
   Conclusions 29
   Other Considerations 30

Chapter II —
Legal Implications of an ISO 9001-based QMS 33
Key Points 34
ISO 9001—The Model 35
Registration Process Pitfalls 36
Liability Exposure 37
Lines of Questioning 39
Summary 44

Scenario 3 47
The Case 50
The Attack and Defense 50
Conclusions 52

Chapter III —
Quality Systems and Product Safety 55
Key Points 56
Focus on the Product 57
ISO 9000 Registration Is Not Enough 57
Product Safety 57
ISO 9001/2/3 and Product Safety 59
ISO 9004-1 and Product Safety 60
The ISO 9000 Paper Trail 61
Summary 69

Chapter IV —
Beyond ISO 9001/2/3...A Preventive Program 73
Key Points 74
Building the Framework of a Preventive Law Program 75
Records Management and Documentation 75
Product Design, Including Risk Assessment/Management 77
Product Design and Product Software 81
Warnings and Instructions 85
Postsale Obligations 88
Component Parts 90
Summary 94

Chapter V —
ISO 9000 & the Harmonization of National Laws **97**

Key Points 98
ISO 9000 & European Law 99
ISO 9000 and International Law 106
ISO 9000 and US Law 107
ISO 9000 & Global Medical Device Regulation 111
ISO 14000—Environmental Management Systems 113
QS-9000 & the Automotive Industry 114
Summary 116

Appendices:

A ISO 9001—An Overview of the Clauses
...and Their Meaning **119**
  1 Scope 119
  2 Normative reference... 119
  3 Definitions 120
  4 Quality system requirements............................... 120
      4.1 Management responsibility 120
      4.2 Quality system 123
      4.3 Contract review 124
      4.4 Design control 125
      4.5 Document and data control 128
      4.6 Purchasing 128
      4.7 Control of customer-supplied product 130
      4.8 Product identification and traceability 130
      4.9 Process control 130
      4.10 Inspection and testing 131
      4.11 Control of inspection, measuring and test
             equipment 132
      4.12 Inspection and test status 133
      4.13 Control of nonconforming product 133
      4.14 Corrective and preventive action 133
      4.15 Handling, storage, packaging, preservation
             and delivery... 134
      4.16 Control of quality records 135

4.17   Internal quality audits 135
4.18   Training 136
4.19   Servicing 136
4.20   Statistical techniques 136
B   EU Directive—The Product Liability Directive **137**
Council Directive of 25 July 1985 137
C   EU Directive—The Product Safety Directive **149**
Council Directive 92/59/EEC of 29 June 1992 on
General Product Safety 149
D   Japanese Law—
Guide to the Product Liability Law (Law No. 85, 1994) **169**
1   Introduction of the Product Liability System 169
2   What is Product Liability? 170
The Product Liability Law (Law No. 85, 1994) **176**
Article 1 [Purpose] 176
Article 2 [Definitions] 176
Article 3 [Product Liability] 177
Article 4 [Exemptions] 177
Article 5 [Time Limitations] 177
Article 6 [Application of Civil Code] 178
E   Sources for More Information **179**

About the Author

JAMES W. KOLKA, PHD, JD

Dr. Kolka is an experienced lawyer, teacher, administrator and quality and environmental management systems expert. He has been a member of the Wisconsin Bar Association for 35 years. Dr. Kolka received his BS in Political Science/Economics/Chemistry from the University of Wisconsin-Eau Claire; his JD from the University of Wisconsin-Madison, with a background in product liability and environmental law; and his PhD in Political Science and International Affairs from the University of Kansas.

For the past seven years, Dr. Kolka has been working extensively in the quality and environmental management system fields, with particular emphasis on the ISO 9000 and ISO 14000 series in the US and their role within the European Union (EU) marketplace. He developed a comprehensive preventive law program that meshes the ISO 9000 quality management system series with the ISO 14000 series for environmental management systems, with the goal of reducing a company's exposure to product liability, environmental liability, product safety and services liability lawsuits in the EU and US markets.

One of Dr. Kolka's strengths and specialties is program development. He has developed regulatory compliance (CE-marking) programs for medical device and machinery companies that export products to the EU. In addition, he has developed corporate management programs designed to integrate systems aimed at reducing liability exposure using ISO 9000 and/or ISO 14000 management system structures. These integrated approaches are being used by companies importing products into the US from the EU, Eastern Europe and the Commonwealth of Independent States and Latin America as well as domestic companies selling products and services in the US.

In terms of teaching and offering his expertise on issues relating to legal liability, EU technical standards, ISO 9000, ISO 14000, exporting and competitiveness, Dr. Kolka has conducted more than 200 training seminars and workshops for North American, European, Asian and Latin American companies; has presented papers on these issues at ASQ and other conferences; and has written several books and more than 175 articles on topics relating to the ISO 9000 and ISO 14000 standards, CE-marking and legal liability. His most recent books are two sections of *Managing for Products Liability Avoidance*, 2nd Edition, 1996; two chapters in the *ISO 9000 Handbook*, 3rd Edition, 1996; *The European Machinery Directive: Compliance Manual for Trade*, 1995, written with Bruce McIntosh; *EC Medical Devices Report*, 1992, written with Gregory Scott and David Link; and *European Community Product Liability and Product Safety Directives*, 1992, written with Gregory Scott.

As an original member of *THE INFORMED OUTLOOK*'s Editorial Advisory Board, Dr. Kolka has been contributing a series of articles to that publication on CE-marking to the EU's medical devices directives, on the FDA's new Quality System Regulation (QSR) and on the Mutual Recognition Agreement between the EU and US recognizing each other's conformity assessment systems.

Presently, Dr. Kolka is a senior consultant with EXCEL Partnership, Inc., where he has designed and developed instructional courses on the FDA's QSR, CE-marking for medical devices and CE-marking for machinery for EXCEL, which he and other EXCEL instructors are teaching around the US and in Europe. He is also developing new preventive law programs using QMS and EMS structures to reduce liability exposure.

Dr. Kolka's academic and professional experience spans more than 35 years. During this time, he has served as a full professor at several universities, has served as Vice President for Academic Affairs at Drake University and in the University System of Georgia and has held senior management positions in the University of Wisconsin System. He developed the University of Wisconsin's Statewide Adult Extended Degree Program and was instrumental in creating the Center for International Standards and Quality (CISQ) at Georgia Tech. Dr. Kolka has developed new interdisciplinary research/teaching models and programs, conducted extensive strategic planning and managed multimillion dollar budgets.

In addition, Dr. Kolka has served as a Ford Foundation Research Fellow for the University of Kansas in Costa Rica and as a Fellow with the American Council on Education (ACE) in Washington, DC, where he also served on ACE's National Commission on Education Credit and Credentials. Presently, he serves on the advisory panel for the Georgia Tech Center for International Business, Education and Research and as Executive in Residence at Georgia Tech's Ivan Allen College of Management, Policy and International Affairs in Atlanta. Dr. Kolka also acts as a standards expert for the European/American Chamber of Commerce Trans-Atlantic Business Dialogue (TABD) and recently chaired ASQ's CE-Marking Conference.

About the Publishers

ASQ

The American Society for Quality is a society of individual and organizational members dedicated to the ongoing development, advancement and promotion of quality concepts, principles and techniques. The Society serves 133,000 individual and 1,100 corporate members.

INFORM

INFORM—International Forum for Management Systems, Inc.— founded in 1995, was established with the goal of providing accurate and timely information and guidance on the use of ISO 9000, QS-9000, ISO 14000 and related international management system standards by way of newsletters, books, training videotapes and other informational and educational media.

More than a decade ago, INFORM executives and directors began analyzing, writing and delivering information and training on the voluntary management system standards that were developing in the international business marketplace. Initially, this work concentrated on ISO 9000 with the development of a lead auditor training program that is still in use in several prominent training organizations today. By 1991, our executives were helping to design and develop publications on ISO 9000 and (beginning in 1994) on ISO 14000 that were to set the standard for materials in this rapidly expanding area of management system standards.

Since 1995, INFORM has focused on these efforts. With the start of INFORM's series of Management Systems Basic booklets — question and answer style books on ISO 9000, QS-9000 and ISO 14000 — in January 1996 and the May 1996 launching of *THE INFORMED*

OUTLOOK newsletter, INFORM has been providing publications to meet the business community's quality and environmental system needs. INFORM's ongoing involvement in the development of training videotapes on ISO 9000, QS-9000 and ISO 14000 is providing companies with effective training tools for a broad range of employee needs. *ISO 9000...A Legal Perspective* is the first full-length book produced by INFORM in what we hope to be a long line of useful, effective management system business books.

All the expertise gained through more than a decade of hard work in bringing usable, timely and accurate information on the standards has given INFORM a perspective and focus that few companies can claim. Our business is the provision of information on international managment system standards and their application to prevailing business practices.

Copies of this book may be purchased from either of the copublishers. Contact information is listed in Appendix E, Sources for More Information.

Acknowledgments

A loyal cadre of colleagues were especially helpful in the development of this book. Thank you.

To Robin and Jim Gildersleeve of INFORM for their vision, enthusiasm, support and creative input. To Jim Mroz of INFORM for his excellent suggestions and assistance. To Kevin Baynes of INFORM for his outstanding work and unique perspective on design, layout and content enhancement. To Roger Holloway of ASQ Press for his strong commitment to this project.

To my wife Sandra, my daughter Jeanmarie, and my son Jamey.

Foreword

The ISO 9000 series of quality assurance and quality management system standards began its second generation with the 1994 revisions and is growing rapidly as a fact of life in global business and in the management of American businesses. Since then, the creation of the ISO 9001-based *QS-9000 Quality System Requirements* by the Big Three US automotive manufacturers, the adaptation of ISO 9001 by the Federal Aviation Administration, the use of ISO 9000 in procurement contracts by NATO, the US Department of Defense, Army, Navy and Air Force, as well as the assimilation of ISO 9001 by the Food and Drug Administration to regulate medical device design and manufacture, all point to ISO 9000 as a growing dynamic governing US business relationships between customers and their suppliers. The affect on international trade is even more profound. Thus, ISO 9000 is perforce a matter of interest and concern for attorneys.

From various discussions I have had over the past few years, it has become apparent to me that quality professionals and attorneys only understand each other's worlds to a degree that often is fuzzy at best. On one hand, many quality consultants have sold ISO 9000 registration as "a great defense in the event of a lawsuit", without understanding the legal implications of such statements to their clients or to themselves. On the other hand, some consultants have complained about attorneys who have commented that guidance documents such as ISO 9004-1 are to be considered components of a series, along with compliance standards such as ISO 9001 or ISO 9002, and can be considered by the courts when establishing a manufacturer's "duty of care."

In a similar manner, attorneys' understanding of the ISO 9000 series ranges widely. There are some attorneys who are proponents of ISO 9001 registration for law firms to improve their quality management vis-à-vis meeting their clients' needs. There are also attorneys who are suspicious of any standard that stipulates additional documentation, and many attorneys who do not understand the relationship between the European Union's ISO 9001/2 conformity assessment procedures for new approach directives and product-specific requirements for CE-marking. In all fairness, the confusion derives in part from the evolving applications of the ISO 9000 series in regulated and unregulated commercial environments.

While confusion about the rapidly growing use of quality management systems and their various applications is normal, misunderstanding isn't productive. My objective in this book is to reduce the misunderstanding and provide a measure of clarification to several parties—lawyers and their clients, quality professionals and their clients or their companies, interested observers and the curious.

ISO 9000…A Legal Perspective

James W. Kolka, PhD, JD

ISO 9000…
A Legal Perspective

Introduction

Increasingly over the next several years, ISO 9000 will enter the day-to-day world of lawyers. Defense attorneys will need to know what it is, how it operates, how it might affect their clients, the types of legal exposures and legal protections it offers or creates and how to go about defending clients in the event of a lawsuit. Plaintiff's attorneys will want to know what it is, how it operates and its purpose, and they will want to determine if it provides a useful vantage from which to attack a prospective defendant and build an effective case in the event of a lawsuit. As we will see, ISO 9000 may prove in some instances to be important even though neither the plaintiff nor the defendant knew of its existence prior to the lawsuit. *Note: The ISO 9000 standards are adopted by each nation individually as the standards are translated into the language of the adopting nation. In the US, the adopted name is "ANSI/ASQC Q9001". This adoption often is referred to generically as "ISO 9001".*

For example, an article entitled "Lawyers Wise Up to ISO 9000" by John R. Broomfield in the January-February 1996 (Volume 13, Number 12) issue of *Compliance Engineering* describes a case resulting from the collapse of a chaise lounge that caused the plaintiff to reinjure a knee that was healing from recent reconstructive surgery. The manufacturer had allowed an improperly fastened leg to leave the production line. Shortly after delivery by the manufacturer to the retailer (where final assembly occurred), the leg broke and the plaintiff fell to the floor. The retailer attempted to pass blame back to the manufacturer, asserting that the assembly instructions were incomplete and confusing. Plaintiff's counsel argued that the manufacturer had ignored the American national standard for quality systems (ANSI/ASQ Q9001) and that the retailer did not document its training or inspections. The case was settled before trial with the plaintiff receiving a total of $55,000 from the manufacturer and retailer.

The preceding example involved companies that were not registered to ISO 9001, and yet they were held accountable to the clauses of an ISO 9001-based quality assurance system (Clause 4.10, Inspection and Testing and Clause 4.18, Training). Attorneys also are beginning to explore the documentation of companies registered to ISO 9001/2/3. For example, several corporate counsels have reported that plaintiffs' attorneys are asking for copies of audits, especially internal audits. In all likelihood, these attorneys are searching for "smoking guns" among reports of nonconformances (e.g., remarks that suggest something is dangerous or unsafe) that could be used to support a liability lawsuit. While most of this search for information may yield little useful material, it does point to the need for instruction in writing about nonconformities.

The growing significance of ISO 9000 to lawyers and to litigation will become obvious as we proceed. To a certain degree it fits one of Sun Tsu's offensive strategy axioms in his 2,500-year-old classic, *The Art of War:* "Know the enemy and know yourself; in a hundred battles you will never be in peril." Perhaps it should be turned about a few degrees and given a modern twist: "If you don't know ISO 9000 as it relates to your client, you could easily be in peril!"

ISO 9001 registration is a significant accomplishment for a company. It requires implementation of a system with fully documented processes and requires the recording of work results that demonstrate performance to documentation. ISO 9001 represents a powerful methodology and is backed up by a paper trail validating a strong management system in the event of a lawsuit. Conversely, it also can represent a significant degree of exposure if the paper trail reveals weak controls that are not able to document a sound quality assurance system. The good news and the bad news are identical; a paper trail exists in the event of a lawsuit.

This book will explore ISO 9000 from a lawyer's perspective: its origins; its structure; the interrelationships of the different ISO 9000 quality management standards; its growing function in the marketplace in the US, European Union (EU) and global economies; its growing use in regulated sectors; its relationship to product safety; its product liability implications; and its possible impact on corporate legal offices and law firms in the future.

Scenarios

In the case described in the January-February 1996 issue of *Compliance Engineering* (John R. Broomfield, "Lawyers Wise Up to ISO 9000", *Compliance Engineering*, Volume 13, Number 1), the lawsuit was settled out of court for $55,000. Neither one of the companies being sued was registered to ISO 9001/2/3, yet they were challenged for ignoring those quality system standards. At present, there are no court cases on record where a company has been challenged by attorneys using the ISO 9000 series of standards where the case has ended in a court decision. It is entirely possible that, as use of the standards proliferates, companies with and without quality systems will be challenged using the ISO 9000 standards.

It is premature to conjecture what may or may not happen if and when such cases do make it to—and are decided in—the courts, but it may prove constructive to look at three case scenarios where companies are met with the legal challenge of having their quality systems (or lack thereof) compared with and contrasted to the ISO 9000 standards. These scenarios are intended to introduce concepts pertinent to the construction of a quality management system from a legal perspective and to illustrate how those concepts may come into play in a court of law. Understanding these concepts and how quality systems may be attacked using them will lead to an understanding of how to formulate a defense against such attacks.

Scenario 1

Consider a company with no formal quality system that manufactures a product with a relatively low level of associated risk. The company has a high level of customer satisfaction and is always working to improve its products.

This particular company, CoolCorp, manufactures residential air conditioners. CoolCorp designs and produces most of its components at its production facility, while certain key components are bought-in and incorporated into the air conditioners. CoolCorp also delivers, installs and services its air conditioners.

One key bought-in component is an electrical connector that supplies electricity to the compressor. CoolCorp buys its connectors from two different vendors ("suppliers" in ISO 9000 terminology), one of which has only recently begun to sell to CoolCorp.

The Case

One air conditioner that CoolCorp installed caught fire when its air compressor overheated and burned down the house that it was supposed to be cooling. Luckily, the family escaped the fire with only minor injuries. The family's insurance company sued CoolCorp for the cost of replacing the house. The basis of the case is that, had CoolCorp implemented an ISO 9001-based quality system, it could have prevented the compressor problem and the fire.

The Attack and Defense

The plaintiff's attorney is familiar with ISO 9000 and quality management system principles and practices. The attorney decides to attack CoolCorp's lack of a formal quality system by asking questions designed to contrast CoolCorp's methods of design, production, delivery, installation and servicing with the practices of an ISO 9001-based quality assurance system.

One area of contrast with ISO 9001 is Clause 4.4, Design Control, which states:

> The supplier [i.e., company] shall establish and maintain *documented procedures to control and verify the design of the product* in order to ensure that the specified requirements are met. [Emphasis added.]

The thrust of this element is that procedures need to be documented. Though CoolCorp has a highly experienced electrical engineer who performs excellent work, there are no written design control procedures. The electrical engineer incorporated new electrical connectors into CoolCorp's existing line of air conditioners. The connectors met every one of CoolCorp's specifications and worked flawlessly in the engineer's tests. However, there was no documentation to prove that the connectors were indeed tested to specification or that there was even a procedure for testing and incorporating components. CoolCorp does have the word of the engineer and other employees, but it has no hard data.

Another area of contrast is Clause 4.9, Process Control, which reads:

> The supplier shall identify and plan the production, installation and servicing processes [that] affect quality and shall ensure that these processes are carried out under controlled conditions.

The main focus of this clause is that a company with an ISO 9001-based quality system must have documented procedures to control production, installation and servicing procedures.

CoolCorp's electrical engineer did advise the production manager for these air conditioners that the new electrical components needed to be connected to the air compressors in a slightly different way. The production manager did show the line employees how to install the new type of connector and had the electrical engineer inspect the first few air conditioners and test them for quality. However, none of these processes was formalized and documented.

Further, these excerpts from Clause 4.16, Control of Quality Records, state:

- The supplier shall *establish and maintain documented procedures*

- *Quality records shall be maintained to demonstrate conformance* to specified requirements and the effective operation of the quality system

- All *quality records* shall be legible and *shall be stored and retained* in such a way that they are readily retrievable [Emphasis added.]

Though CoolCorp's employees fastidiously carried out sensible procedures to assure the quality and safety of their products, CoolCorp kept no records of quality procedures.

Another area of contrast is Clause 4.18, Training, which reads:

> The supplier shall establish and maintain documented

procedures for identifying training needs and provide for the training of all personnel performing activities affecting quality. Personnel performing specific assigned tasks shall be qualified on the basis of appropriate education, training and/or experience, as required. Appropriate records shall be maintained.

CoolCorp's employees are highly trained and qualified to do their jobs. Each employee is screened by the manager of the area into which the employee is hired. Employees undergo a mentoring process whereby experienced employees guide new employees through appropriate processes and procedures. However, CoolCorp has no documentation to back up this training process.

Conclusions

No one yet knows how a judge or jury might respond to a similar line of attack by plaintiff's attorney contrasting ISO 9001 with a company lacking a formal quality management system. However, it is obvious that one of the most prominent distinguishing features of an ISO 9001-based quality management system (QMS) is that the system is documented and therefore evidence of quality assurance procedures exists. ISO 9001/2/3 requires that processes and procedures are documented and carefully maintained. It is possible that, had CoolCorp documented its QMS, it could have demonstrated to a judge and jury that care was taken to ensure the quality and safety of its products.

Note that any records kept could serve as evidence of negligence on the part of CoolCorp if its procedures and processes were negligent. Implementation of an ISO 9001-based QMS will not automatically result in improved processes. The ISO 9000 series is merely a tool; and as with any tool, results vary with its application. Poor application of any tool will yield poor results.

The best method of defense for a company challenged with a lawsuit on the basis that the company ignored the ISO 9000 series is to muster as much evidence as possible to demonstrate a corporate commitment to quality and product safety. Quality is the product of systematic application of good management practices at all levels of a corporation. Product safety is the result of corporate emphasis on safety throughout all facets of a product's life cycle, from design through disposal.

Properly used, the ISO 9000 series can help any company implement and improve processes and procedures to assure quality. Combined with a strong corporate commitment to safety and quality, an ISO 9001-based QMS may provide the necessary documented commitment to quality and product safety.

Other Considerations

What if the plaintiff's attorney decided to file a product liability lawsuit based on alleged neglect or poor manufacturing processes? How could the ISO 9000 series affect the defense's case?

- It's possible that a properly implemented ISO 9001-based QMS, with a strong corporate emphasis on quality, safety and continual improvement, may have aided CoolCorp in avoiding a lawsuit altogether.

- It's possible that a properly implemented ISO 9001-based QMS, with a strong corporate emphasis on quality, safety and continual improvement, may have provided sufficient documented evidence to aid CoolCorp's legal defense.

- It's possible that a properly implemented ISO 9001-based QMS, with a strong corporate emphasis on quality, safety and continual improvement, may have had no effect on a judge or jury's decision in such a case.

- It's possible that a *poorly* implemented system, designed to have minimal impact on management and corporate procedures, may produce records that could come to light in the discovery phase to document CoolCorp's negligence.

Chapter 1

Introduction to ISO 9000

OVERVIEW

ISO 9000's influence on US business is growing, and its importance to lawyers and litigation is increasing with that growth. This chapter focuses on the origins of ISO 9000, the elements of the ISO 9000 series of standards, its growing function in the US and the reasons why companies are registering to ISO 9001/2/3.

KEY POINTS

❖ ISO 9000 was created by the International Organization for Standardization, which is based in Geneva, Switzerland. The first ISO 9000 standards were released in 1987 and the family was revised in 1994.

❖ ISO 9000's roots can be traced to the US Department of Defense's "MIL-Q-9858-A Quality Program Requirements" and the British Standards Institution's BS 5750.

❖ In simple terms, ISO 9001 tells you to document what you do, do what you document, ensure the process is effective (make changes to the documentation as necessary) and make the results available.

❖ ISO 9000 quality management system programs contain specified quality management requirements that are documented and evaluated on a periodic basis. For better or worse, there is a paper trail.

❖ Although the ISO 9000 series consists of more than 20 standards, the series contains five key standards: three conformance standards and two guidance documents. A site registers its quality system to one of the conformance standards: ISO 9001, ISO 9002 or ISO 9003.

❖ The most important guidance standards are ISO 9000-1 and ISO 9004-1. ISO 9004-1 is most often ignored, which is unfortunate because it raises liability issues and exposures that deserve serious attention.

❖ Registrations are fueled by governmental pressures to increase competitiveness, customer requirements and other market pressures for increased quality and internal pressures to increase productivity and profits.

The Origins of ISO 9000

While it seems that the ISO 9000 series of standards, created by the International Organization for Standardization (ISO), burst upon the world in the past decade, the origins of a contractual quality assurance system can be traced back to 1963 when the US Department of Defense (DoD) published its "MIL-Q-9858A Quality Program Requirements".

In 1979, the Geneva-based ISO formed Technical Committee (TC) 176 (an international committee that includes US representation) to bring about "standardization in the field of generic quality management, including quality systems, quality assurance and generic supporting technologies, including standards which provide guidance on the selection and use of standards." (Source: International Organization for Standardization, *ISO Momento 1989*, Geneva, Switzerland). The TC's work was influenced by the US DoD quality standards and, in particular by BS 5750, the quality assurance standard developed by the British Standards Institution in 1979, which was also modeled after US DoD quality standards.

In its simplest and most basic form, an ISO 9001/2/3-based quality assurance system contains a series of documents that require a company to:

- Document what it does
- Perform to that documentation
- Ensure the process is effective
- Record the results of the work.

For attorneys, it is important to know that ISO 9000 quality management programs contain specified quality management elements, which are documented and evaluated on a periodic basis. For better or worse, there is a paper trail.

Elements of the ISO 9000 Series

At present there are more than 20 standards within the ISO 9000 series, of which there are five key standards that concern most companies. Two are guidance documents and three are conformance standards. Registration, the act of having a quality system verified as being in conformance with a set of requirements by an appropriate third-party authority, occurs to the conformance standards.

Key Guidance Standards

ISO 9000-1: Quality Management and
Quality Assurance Standards—Guidelines
for Selection and Use

This standard should be reviewed first by companies contemplating registration. It provides a basic explanation of the ISO 9000 series, definitions of key terms and guidance on the selection and use of each conformance standard.

ISO 9004-1: Quality Management and
Quality System Elements—Guidelines

While this standard should be reviewed before implementing a quality system to a conformance standard, such as ISO 9001 or ISO 9002, most often it is ignored. This is unfortunate because it offers significant guidance on implementing a QMS and makes statements about controls that relate to liability issues and exposures that deserve serious attention. ISO 9004-1 provides detailed guidance on the application of conformance standards to the development of internal QMSs and it raises many questions that should be considered when creating these systems. The structure of ISO 9004-1 is outlined in Table 1-1 on pages 15-16.

Conformance Standards

The three conformance standards are the standards to which companies become registered. Some important facts about these conformance standards are:

- They are generic in structure (i.e., they can be applied to quality systems in a wide range of industries—from manufacturing to service).

- They are prescriptive in nature (e.g., "a supplier [company] *shall* define and document how the requirements *shall* be met)."

- They contain generic clauses, all of which must be successfully addressed.

Table 1-1: The Structure of ISO 9004-1 Quality Management and Quality System Elements—Guidelines

1 Scope

2 Normative References

3 Definitions
3.1 Organization
3.2 Customer
3.3 Requirements of Society
3.4 Quality Plan
3.5 Product
3.6 Service

4 Management Responsibility
4.1 General
4.2 Quality Policy
4.3 Quality Objectives
4.4 Quality Systems

5 Quality System Elements
5.1 Extent of Application
5.2 Structure of the Quality System
   - General
   - Responsibility & authority
   - Organizational structure
   - Resources and personnel
   - Operational procedures
   - Configuration management
5.3 Documentation of the Quality System
   - Quality policies and procedures
   - Quality system documentation
   - Quality plans
   - Quality records
5.4 Auditing and the Quality System
   - General
   - Audit program
   - Extent of audits
   - Audit reporting
   - Follow-up action
5.5 Review and Evaluation of the Quality System
5.6 Quality Improvement

6 Financial Considerations of Quality Systems
6.1 General
6.2 Approaches to Financial Reporting of Quality System Activities
   - General
   - Approaches
   a) Quality-costing approach
   b) Process-cost approach
   c) Quality-loss approach
6.3 Reporting

7 Quality in Marketing
7.1 Marketing Requirements
7.2 Defining Product Specification
7.3 Customer Feedback Information

8 Quality in Specification and Design
8.1 Contribution of Specification and Design to Quality
8.2 Design Planning and Objectives
8.3 Product Testing and Measurement
8.4 Design Review
   - General
   - Elements of design reviews
   a) Items pertaining to customer needs and satisfaction
   b) Items pertaining to product specification
   c) Items pertaining to process specification
   - Design verification
8.5 Design Qualification and Validation
8.6 Final Design Review and Production Release
8.7 Market-Readiness Review
8.8 Design-Change Control
8.9 Design Requalification
8.10 Configuration Management in Design

9 Quality in Purchasing
9.1 General
9.2 Requirements for Specifications, Drawings and Purchase Documents
9.3 Selection of Acceptable Subcontractors
9.4 Agreement on Quality Assurance

Table 1-1: The Structure of ISO 9004-1 (cont)

9.5 Agreement on Verification Methods

9.6 Provisions for Settlement of Disputes

9.7 Receiving Inspection Planning and Control

9.8 Quality Records Related to Purchasing

10 Quality of Process
10.1 Planning for Process Control
10.2 Process Capability
10.3 Supplies, Utilities and Environment
10.4 Handling

11 Control of Processes
11.1 General
11.2 Materials Control, Traceability and Identification
  • Material control
  • Traceability
  • Identification
11.3 Equipment Control and Maintenance
11.4 Process-Control Management
11.5 Documentation
11.6 Process-Change Control
11.7 Control of Verification Status
11.8 Control of Nonconforming Product

12 Product Verification
12.1 Incoming Materials and Parts
12.2 In-Process Verification
12.3 Finished Process Verification

13 Control of Inspection, Measuring and Test Equipment
13.1 Measurement Control
13.2 Elements of Control
13.3 Subcontractor Measurement Controls
13.4 Corrective Action
13.5 Outside Testing

14 Control of Nonconforming Product
14.1 General
14.2 Identification
14.3 Segregation

14.4 Review
14.5 Disposition
14.6 Action
14.7 Avoidance of Recurrence

15 Corrective Action
15.1 General
15.2 Assignment of Responsibility
15.3 Evaluation of Importance
15.4 Investigation of Possible Causes
15.5 Analysis of Problem
15.6 Elimination of Causes
15.7 Process Controls
15.8 Permanent Changes

16 Postproduction Activities
16.1 Storage
16.2 Delivery
16.3 Installation
16.4 Servicing
16.5 After Sales
16.6 Market Feedback

17 Quality Records
17.1 General
17.2 Quality Records
17.3 Quality-Records control

18 Personnel
18.1 Training
  • General
  • Executive and management personnel
  • Technical personnel
  • Process supervisors and operating personnel
18.2 Qualification
18.3 Motivation
  • General
  • Applicability
  • Quality awareness
  • Measuring quality

19 Product Safety

20 Use of Statistical Methods
20.1 Applications
20.2 Statistical Techniques

ANNEX A (Informative)
Bibliography

Table 1-2: The 20 Clauses and Subclauses of ISO 9001, Section 4, Quality System Requirements

4.1 Management Responsibility
Quality Policy
Organization
- Responsibility and Authority
- Resources
- Management Representative
Management Review

4.2 Quality System
General
Quality-System Procedures
Quality Planning

4.3 Contract Review
General
Review
Amendment to Contract
Records

4.4 Design Control*
General
Design and Development Planning
Organizational and Technical
     Interfaces
Design Input
Design Output
Design Review
Design Verification
Design Validation
Design Changes

4.5 Document and Data Control
General
Document and Data Approval and
     Issue
Document and Data Changes

4.6 Purchasing**
General
Evaluation of Subcontractors
Purchasing Data
Verification of Purchased Product
Customer Verification of
     Subcontracted Product

4.7 Control of Customer-Supplied Product

4.8 Product Identification and Traceability

4.9 Process Control**

4.10 Inspection and Testing
General
Receiving Inspection and Testing**
In-Process Inspection and Testing**
Final Inspection and Testing
Inspection and Test Records

4.11 Control of Inspection, Measuring and Test Equipment
General
Control Procedure

4.12 Inspection and Test Status

4.13 Control of Nonconforming Product
General
Review and Disposition of Non-
     conforming Product

4.14 Corrective and Preventive Action
General**
Corrective Action
Preventive Action**

4.15 Handling, Storage, Packaging, Preservation and Delivery
General
Handling
Storage
Packaging
Preservation
Delivery

4.16 Control of Quality Records

4.17 Internal Quality Audits

4.18 Training

4.19 Servicing

4.20 Statistical Techniques
Identification of Need
Procedures

*   Denotes clause of ISO 9001 not contained in ISO 9002 and ISO 9003.

**   Denotes clauses or subclauses of ISO 9001 not contained in ISO 9003.

- Sites generally are registered by a professionally accredited third-party (registrar) that approves the quality system if the conformance standard's criteria have been successfully met—as judged by the registrar's professionally certified auditors.

- Once registered, each system is subject to periodic internal audits, surveillance audits by the registrar and usually a full-scale re-audit approximately every three years.

- If the company or its quality system should change dramatically (e.g., expansion, acquisition, change of focus), appropriate adjustments would be necessary that could require an added surveillance audit or complete re-registration of the altered system.

ISO 9001: Quality Systems—Model for
Quality Assurance in Design, Development,
Production, Installation and Servicing

This is the most comprehensive of the three conformance standards. It includes everything from design through production to storage, delivery and servicing. ISO 9002 and ISO 9003 do not contain all requirements of ISO 9001. The 20 clauses of ISO 9001 are outlined in Table 1-2 on page 17, with the clauses/subclauses not in ISO 9002 and ISO 9003 noted.

ISO 9002: Quality Systems—Model for
Quality Assurance in Production, Installation
and Servicing

This conformance standard is identical to ISO 9001 except that it does not include the design function. It applies to a wide range of facilities that manufacture to external design specifications and facilities that make product lines destined for end-use manufacturers; e.g., sheet steel and sheet aluminum. This model also is used by companies that wish to be registered to ISO 9001 but are not prepared to submit their design processes to the scrutiny of ISO 9001 registration assessment. This raises potentially serious legal questions about the substance and quality of the design function. For example, the plaintiff's attorney in a liability claim might find it useful to explore the rationale of an ISO 9002-based quality assurance system that excluded the design function in ISO 9001 (Clause 4.4, Design Control) and ask whether such an exclusion indicates a lack of design control and low level of attention to product safety. The clauses of ISO 9002 are outlined in Table 1-2 on page 17.

Table 1-3: The ISO 9000 Guidance Standards

Number	Name	Revision/Status
Standards of Use in Preparation for Registration		
ISO 8402	Quality Management and Quality Assurance—Vocabulary	1994
ISO 9000-1	Guidelines for Selection and Use	1994
ISO 9000-2	Generic Guidelines for the Application of ISO 9001/2/3	1993 (FDIS)
ISO 10002	Quality Management Principles	
(9004-8)	and Guidelines for Their Application	CD
Standards Addressing Application in Specific Industries or Technologies		
ISO 9004-2	Guidelines for Services	1991 (1993 reissue)
ISO 9004-3	Guidelines for Processed Materials	1993
ISO 9000-3	Guidelines for the Application of ISO 9001 in the	1991 (1993 reissue)
	Development, Supply and Maintenance of Software	(FDIS)
ISO 10015	Guidelines for Training	DIS
ISO/TRXX	Automotive Quality System Requirements	Work begun 1997
Standards Pertaining to an Existing Element of ISO 9001		
ISO 9000-4	Application for Dependability Program Management	1993
ISO 10005	Guidelines for Quality Assurance Plans (9004-5)	1994
ISO 10007	Guidelines for Configuration Management (9004-7)	1995
ISO 10011	Guidelines for Auditing Quality Systems	1994
Part 1	Auditing	1990 (1993 reissue)
Part 2	Qualification Criteria for Quality System Auditors	1991 (1993 reissue)
Part 3	Management of Audit Programs	1991 (1993 reissue)
ISO 10012	Quality Assurance Requirements for Measuring Equipment	
Part 1	Management of Measuring Equipment	1992 (CD)
Part 2	Control of Measurement Processes	1997
ISO 10013	Guidelines for Developing Quality Manuals	1995
ISO 10016	Inspection/Test Records—Guidelines for Presenting Results	WD
Standards Addressing Subject Areas That Go Beyond ISO 9001		
ISO/TR 10002	Quality Management Principles	1997
ISO 10004	Guidelines for Quality Improvement (9004-4)	1993
ISO/TR 10006	Guidelines for Quality in Project Management (9004-6)	1997
ISO 10014	Guideline for Managing the Economics of Quality	FDIS
ISO/TR 10017	Guidelines on the Application of Statistical Techniques	WD

Key: WD—Working Draft; CD—Committee Draft; DIS—Draft International Standard; TR—Technical Report.

Source: ISO

ISO 9003: Quality Systems—Model for
Quality Assurance in Final Inspection and Test

ISO 9003 is the least comprehensive of the three conformance standards and is not widely used since it does not include design or production. It focuses on requirements for final inspection and testing. The clauses of ISO 9003 are outlined in Table 1-2, page 17.

Other Standards

Other useful guidance standards in the ISO 9000 series are identified in Table 1-3 on page 19. New standards are developed and issued periodically. The more prominent standards include subsets to ISO 9000 and ISO 9004—the guidance standards—ISO 10011 (Auditing), ISO 10012 (Measuring Equipment) and ISO 10013 (Quality Manuals).

ISO TC 176 reviews the standards every five years to evaluate performance and consider revisions. The most recent revisions were adopted in 1994 and were fairly modest in scope — management duties were made more explicit, quality planning was added and contract review and design control requirements were expanded. While it is still under discussion, consideration is being given to the adoption of a single conformance standard (ISO 9001) by the year 2000.

Why Companies Register

Early History of ISO 9000 Registrations

In spite of strong ties to US DoD efforts to create quality control among military suppliers, early ISO 9001/2/3 registrations grew rather slowly in the United States compared with global registrations. For example, by March 1995, registration sites had reached 95,600 worldwide while US registrations were approximately 6,000. This should be contrasted to UK registrations at 44,000 and the rest of Europe at 28,000. By November 1997, however, US ISO 9001/2/3 registration certificates surpassed 15,000.

The Big Three US automotive manufacturers (Chrysler, Ford and General Motors) have introduced *Quality System Requirements QS-9000* (an automotive sector-specific quality system requirements standard that includes ISO 9001, Section 4). Because the Big Three have set QS-9000 "certification" as requisite for their suppliers, US registrations are growing rapidly. This requirement affects more than 8,000 automotive suppliers. [Note: Chrysler and General Motors are requiring all their production and service part suppliers to achieve QS-9000 registration by set deadlines, while Ford requires QS-9000 compliance but not third-party registration.]

There are several other reasons for rapid growth of ISO 9001/2/3 registrations (often called certifications in other countries) outside the US. One of the most influential factors was the early development of BS 5750—the predecessor to ISO 9001—in the UK, which spurred ISO 9001/2/3 registrations in a wide variety of sectors, from manufacturing to service industries, not only in the UK but throughout the European Union (EU) and worldwide.

Governmental Pressures

In the EU, the adoption of several comprehensive new approach safety directives—laws—since 1985 and the adoption of a Global Approach to Certification and Testing, which uses ISO 9000 in three of eight conformity assessment modules, has given considerable prominence to the role of ISO 9000 in regulated products. In countries as diverse as Singapore and Ireland, ISO 9000 registration is seen as a key element to competing in the global economy. Consequently, all facilities in Singapore have the full cost of their ISO 9000 registration paid for by the government. In Ireland, up to 80 percent of the costs are paid for by the government, which in turn is subsidized by the EU.

The Marketplace

Although the compliance structure of federal agencies (such as the FDA) is being conceptually harmonized with ISO 9001, or ISO 9001 is being factored into procurement requirements of other US agencies (e.g., DoD and NASA) or of international organizations (e.g., NATO), the significant growth in ISO 9001/2/3 registrations has come about because of demands in the commercial marketplace. Registration is increasingly becoming a requirement for doing business:

● It's good for customers (reduces the need for their own [second-party] quality audits of suppliers).

- It's good for suppliers (able to meet the quality system requirements of many customers with ISO 9000 registration).

- It's a good way to strengthen management system efficiency for both customer and supplier.

For example, Company X, which manufactures washing machines, buys parts and components from a variety of suppliers. To assure consistent quality, Company X conducts periodic supplier audits. If these suppliers were registered to a quality system standard in which Company X had confidence, and they were assessed and registered by an accredited third-party registrar, Company X could accept a supplier's quality system registration (i.e., ISO 9001/2/3) in lieu of performing second-party audits of the supplier.

Clearly, money could be saved by enhancing the customer's confidence in a supplier's quality system. Furthermore, prospective suppliers would know in advance that ISO 9001/2/3 registration is a requirement of doing business with Company X. In addition, Company X could register to ISO 9001/2/3 to improve its own quality on a consistent basis and, if experience is any guide, improve efficiency, cut waste and save money.

Summary

This chapter should leave you with an understanding of what ISO 9000 is, why its influence on businesses around the globe is increasing and why this growing influence will require many lawyers to acquire at least a working knowledge of ISO 9000.

ISO 9000 is a series of international management system standards that have evolved from early military specifications for quality and from the UK's BS 5750 quality assurance standard. The standards, developed with consensus from the international community, are published by ISO. The ISO 9000 standards are generically structured frameworks that can be applied to any industry or activity.

The basic thrust of ISO 9000 is that, to be truly effective and efficient, a company needs to document its quality system, follow its documented procedures and make changes to the system to correct faults and weaknesses and make the results of the documented system available.

One of the most notable aspects of ISO 9001/2/3 is that the system requires extensive documentation of procedures and their results. This means that there is an extensive set of documents that could come into play in the event of litigation. There is a paper trail.

ISO 9000 is comprised of three conformance standards to which companies register and a number of guidance standards, of which ISO 9000-1 and ISO 9004-1 can be considered the most important.

Companies register to ISO 9001/2/3 for a variety of reasons. The primary reasons are: governmental pressure to increase competitiveness and safety and reduce trade barriers, market pressures for increased quality and internal customer requirements pressures to increase productivity and profit.

Scenarios

At present, there are no court cases on record where a company has been challenged by attorneys using the ISO 9000 series standards where the case has ended in a court decision. It is premature to conjecture what may or may not happen if and when such cases do make it to—and are decided in—the courts. This scenario covers some of the possible legal issues using a fictional company and its liability situation.

As discussed in Chapter 1, the ISO 9000 series contains three conformance standards to which companies register their quality systems. ISO 9001 is the most comprehensive standard, while ISO 9002 does not include the design elements of ISO 9001. ISO 9003 addresses only the requirements for detection and control of problems during final inspection and testing. The series also contains guidance documents, including ISO 9000-1 and ISO 9004-1 among others.

Scenario 2

MarineTech designs and manufactures boat engines. One of MarineTech's biggest customers, a manufacturer of motorboats, required MarineTech to implement and register a quality assurance system to ISO 9001 as a condition of a large contract. The company documented its procedures and completed all the technical requirements of ISO 9001, successfully achieving registration. MarineTech then began a practice of preparing its quality system to pass the semiannual surveillance audits to maintain its registration status, thereby retaining its largest contract. The company always went through a phase of internal audits three months prior to its semiannual surveillance audits and then another round of internal audits just prior to the registrar's visit to confirm corrective actions had been taken on the quality system whenever a nonconformance was found.

The customer built large racing boats, requiring motors with lots of horsepower and acceleration capabilities. MarineTech produced a very successful line of engines for these boats, striving to increase their power and decrease their weight to allow for faster acceleration. MarineTech began production of a very fast and lightweight engine, which was also smaller than previous engines. This motor quickly became a top-seller for MarineTech.

What the management of MarineTech did not realize was that some boat manufacturers and specialty shops were purchasing the motors and installing them into smaller ski boats and other pleasure craft. The engines were small enough to be installed into these boats with very little modification, but they were too powerful. This allowed the smaller boats to attain excessive speeds.

The Case

The summer after MarineTech's new engine hit the market, a number of boating accidents occurred when smaller boats using the new engine went out of control, injuring occupants and bystanders and damaging boats and other property. A number of boat owners brought suit against the boat manufacturers and MarineTech.

The Attack and Defense

The plaintiff's attorney was familiar with the ISO 9000 series and quality management principles and practices. The attorney decided to attack MarineTech's quality system using lines of questioning revolving around the requirements of ISO 9001, the manufacturer's "duty of care" to consider all the ISO 9000 standards and other product safety issues raised in ISO 9004-1. The plaintiff's attorney also sought to obtain MarineTech's quality system documentation during the discovery phase of the trial. In this scenario, it is assumed that the plaintiff's attorney was able to obtain copies of MarineTech's quality system documentation. This may or may not take place in future court cases.

One of the first areas that the plaintiff's attorney focused on was product safety in relation to MarineTech's quality policy. Unfortunately for MarineTech, the quality policy made no mention of any commitment by MarineTech to product safety, only to quality and continual improvement.

Product safety is briefly discussed in ISO 9001.

Subclause 4.4.5, Design Control—Design Output states that design output shall:

> c) identify those characteristics of the design that are crucial to the safe and proper functioning of the product (e.g., operating, storage, handling, maintenance and disposal requirements).

MarineTech did identify and document the characteristics of its designs that were crucial to the safe and proper functioning of the product. The quality records documented careful testing of operating tolerances, including specifications for maximum and minimum weight requirements of the boats in which the engines were intended to be used. However, MarineTech should have used this as an opportunity to identify facets of its engine design that would have increased product safety—such as designing the engine to reduce the possibility of misuse or of use other than that intended or providing warnings.

The plaintiff's attorney then focused on product safety as it pertains specifically to ISO 9004-1. In the US, guidance documents such as ISO 9004-1, which contains a section on product safety, help to establish a manufacturer's "duty of care" and can be used by courts to establish evidence of negligence or of a design defect. The plaintiff's attorney discovered that MarineTech's management did not consider ISO 9004-1 during or after its registration.

One area the attorney focused on within ISO 9004-1 was Section 5, Quality-System Elements, Clause 5.1, Extent of Application, which states that the quality system applies to:

> all phases in the life cycle of a product or processes...

Some typical phases are packaging and storage, after sales and disposal or recycling at the end of useful life. MarineTech could produce no documented assessment of the life cycles of its products. Although a number of MarineTech's employees could explain anecdotally the typical life cycle of a boat engine, there was no documentation to demonstrate any attempt to assess the impacts of products after shipment from the factory. During life cycle analysis of the engines, MarineTech would have had the opportunity to at least document consideration of product safety at all phases of the life cycle—and possibly to increase the safety of the products.

Clause 5.1 relates to Clause 5.2, Structure of the Quality System, Subclause 5.2.6, Configuration Management, of ISO 9004-1 which reads:

This discipline is initiated early in the design phase and continues through the whole life-cycle of a product.

Since MarineTech had not determined the life cycle of its engines, it could not demonstrate adequate concern for quality and especially product safety during all phases of an engine's life cycle. As with Subclause 5.1.1, MarineTech would have had the opportunity to at least demonstrate an attempt to increase product safety, from design through disposal; at best, it may have been able to increase product safety.

The plaintiff's attorney examined MarineTech's ISO 9001-registered quality assurance system in relation to the following subclauses of Clause 5.3, Documentation of the Quality System, in ISO 9004-1: 5.3.2, Quality System Documentation; 5.3.3, Quality Plans; and 5.3.4, Quality Records. These subclauses stress the importance of quality system documentation, within which it would behoove MarineTech to document efforts to increase product safety.

In ISO 9004-1, Clause 6.2, Approaches to Financial Reporting of Quality System Activities, Subclause 6.2.2, Approaches, references use of a quality-costing approach to reporting external failure costs resulting from product failure after delivery, such as: "product maintenance and repair, warranties and returns, direct costs and allowances, product recall costs, liability costs." MarineTech had no documentation of consideration given to its postsale product safety liability. Again, at least MarineTech had an opportunity to consider its product safety liabilities and at best to decrease them.

One key clause of ISO 9004-1 is 7.3, Quality in Marketing— Customer Feedback Information, which states:

The marketing function should establish an information-monitoring and feedback system on a continuous basis.

One question for the plaintiff's attorney then becomes obvious: How is your company utilizing product feedback information to update its information on product use and misuse? MarineTech was very much in sync with its industry, yet it had no formally documented feedback system to handle reports of product use and misuse.

Another key subclause of ISO 9004-1 is 8.4.2, Quality in Specification and Design—Elements of Design Reviews, which requires consideration of:

> a) Items pertaining to customer needs and satisfaction
>
> 4) unintended uses and misuses;
>
> b) Items pertaining to product specification
>
> 9) labeling, warnings, identification, traceability requirements, and user instructions;

MarineTech had no documentation of any design reviews with the intention of increasing product safety by considering "unintended uses and misuses" or "labeling, warnings...and user instructions." Many of the previous elements might have helped MarineTech identify key unintended uses and misuses and allowed it to design them out or warn users against those misuses.

To MarineTech's credit, its quality system did attempt to identify the major safety aspects of its products, and it provided ample documentation of rigorous prototyping and testing procedures and their results. However, MarineTech did not document any attention to ISO 9004-1, Section 19, Product Safety, which recommends steps for identifying safety aspects of products in order to enhance safety, including:

> c) analyzing instructions and warnings to the user, maintenance manuals, and labeling and promotional material in order to minimize misinterpretation, particularly regarding intended use and known hazards.

MarineTech provided no safety warnings to its clients or the end users of its motors concerning intended uses of the motors, including minimum and maximum weight limits of the boats that the motors were designed to power.

Conclusions

Again, no one yet knows how a judge or jury might respond to a similar line of attack by a plaintiff's attorney contrasting ISO

9004-1 with a company's sufficient yet not comprehensive quality management system. It is important to note that just as documentation separates a formal quality system from an informal one, documentation of affirmative steps to increase product safety throughout the entire life cycle of a product is one of the key factors that separates a quality assurance system from a QMS. It is possible that such systematic affirmative steps to increase and document product safety as a corporate philosophy or goal may make the difference in a court of law.

It is obvious that simple registration to ISO 9001/2/3 may not be enough to decrease a company's liability. Minimal satisfaction of the requirements of ISO 9001/2/3 will yield a quality assurance system where the focus is on the system, not on the product. To work effectively, product safety commitment must be developed, documented and displayed at all levels of management. ISO 9004-1 can be a useful tool for developing an effective QMS, and as a part of the ISO 9000 series, it helps to establish a manufacturer's "duty of care" to consider it along with the conformance standards.

Once again, product safety documentation is the key. It would behoove any company with a formal quality system to document its commitment to product safety at all levels, from the corporate quality policy through design and postsale obligations.

Other Considerations

ISO 9001 is a conformance standard with quality assurance system requirements that a company must satisfy to achieve and maintain registration. It may be convenient to think of ISO 9001 as a framework or skeleton that may be fleshed out or even armored. Any requirement can be built into that framework of requirements, based on the individual needs of the registered site.

Some QMSs are now incorporating practices and requirements of quality system approaches from around the world, going far beyond the basics of ISO 9001/2/3. One such practice is to include requirements to manufacture products to meet the EU's CE-marking standards—even with no intention of exporting to the EU—because of the advantages of using a technical file to consolidate the product's safety information. Some QMSs now build in requirements to satisfy the EU's Product Liability Directive (see

Appendix B, page 137) or Japanese product liability law (see Appendix D, page 169). The point is that ISO 9001/2/3 is a baseline that can be expanded upon infinitely.

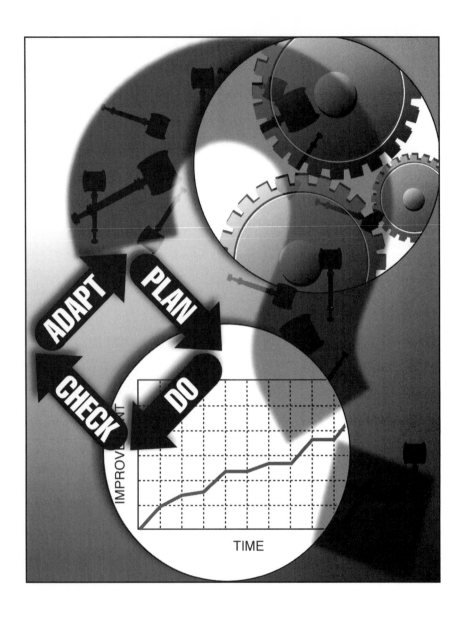

Chapter II

Legal Implications of an ISO 9001-based QMS

OVERVIEW

This chapter deals with some of the legal implications of creating and maintaining an ISO 9001-based quality management system (QMS), as well as the legal exposure a company without a quality system faces when contrasted to the systematic structure of ISO 9001. This chapter will illustrate how a company with a weak quality system or no quality system at all can be attacked using clauses of ISO 9001 to generate lines of questioning.

KEY POINTS

Important: If the absence of a quality system exposes a company to liability lawsuits when its practices and behaviors are contrasted with the structured practices and behaviors of a registered quality system, then ISO 9001/2/3 registration soon may become the price of doing business in the United States. It will become the minimum hurdle for US businesses.

Important: In the event of a lawsuit, if a company has a registered ISO 9001-based QMS, the documentation can be obtained through discovery to determine whether the requirements under Clause 4.4, Design Control, have been satisfactorily addressed and audited. The key for any company's defense will be adequate and effective documentation.

❖ If a company's quality management program is well-constructed and well-documented, it should be able to sustain the scrutiny of a legal challenge. The caliber of documentation will be crucial.

❖ If a company is registered to ISO 9002 because it chose to exclude Design Control from the rigors and scrutiny of registration, it should anticipate potential legal challenges on this point.

❖ If a company has not registered and/or does not have at least an internal QA system, it is vulnerable to a challenge on each and every clause and subclause of ISO 9001.

❖ All participants in the ISO 9001/2/3 quality assurance process are vulnerable to liability exposure. This includes the company itself, the consultants who help construct the quality system, the third-party that serves as the registrar and the auditors employed by the registrar.

❖ For consultants, registrars and auditors, the quality of their professional advice, expertise and competence—or lack thereof—exposes them to the same liability for professional malpractice that affects the activities of doctors and lawyers.

❖ Attorneys should prepare for a veritable explosion of ISO 9001/2/3 registrations in the marketplace because of customer pressures (e.g., the automotive industry and QS-9000). Also, another level of growth will be fueled by the use of ISO 9001/2/3 as a conformity assessment requirement in US- and EU-regulated industries.

ISO 9001—The Model

Quality Management vs. Quality Assurance

The terms quality assurance system (QA system) and quality management system (QMS) are often mistakenly used interchangeably. A QA system affects the activities of a company in fulfilling the requirements for quality. Proper implementation of ISO 9001/2/3 in its most basic form—meeting all the requirements of the 20 clauses of Section 4 and with minimal change to and effect on management—will result in a QA system.

A QMS exceeds a QA system in its scope. Quality management means "all activities of the overall management function that determine the quality policy, objectives and responsibilities and implement them by means such as quality planning, quality control, quality assurance and quality improvement within the quality system." (ISO 8402:1994)

Thus, quality assurance is a subset of quality management. The proper implementation of ISO 9001/2/3 will result in a useful and productive QA system, which will produce a paper trail that may come to light during discovery. But an ISO 9001-based QA system (used minimally) may not be enough when faced with a legal challenge. Yet, a fully implemented QMS with emphasis on safety and quality throughout all aspects of the company may prove adequate for a legal defense.

Elements of a Full Quality Assurance System

Because ISO 9001 is the most comprehensive ISO 9000 conformance standard, it provides the most complete snapshot of all the requirements of an ISO 9000-based quality management program. If, as a growing number of lawyers anticipate, ISO 9001/2/3 registration becomes a minimum legal hurdle for surviving in the marketplace, ISO 9001 represents the most complex model of that hurdle. It is the baseline QA system to which companies with no quality system may be contrasted.

Registration Process Pitfalls

Note: This text refers to ISO 9001/2/3 registration and registered companies; however, it is not necessary for a documented QMS to be registered. Companies may implement an ISO 9001/2/3-based QMS and then "self-declare" that system to be ISO 9001/2/3-compliant. An unregistered ISO 9001/2/3-based QMS may be as or more effective than a registered system, but many industries and customers require the objective, third-party verification of conformance imposed by registration. For the purposes of this book, the focus will be on ISO 9001/2/3 registration, not "self-declaration".

Commitment Levels—Full vs. Partial

As noted earlier, the ISO 9000 standards and their elements are generic in structure. Consequently, it is the application of these generic elements by a company to its structure and operations that makes each system unique. If a company examines the 20 clauses of ISO 9001 and chooses this as an opportunity to create a more efficient, cost-effective QA system, it can do so. Or if a company chooses to make the minimum number of changes to satisfy system requirements—with minimal impact on management—it can do so. A company decides for itself whether ISO 9000 will be used optimally or minimally, thus the results in terms of quality system effectiveness can be widely divergent.

Conflict-of-Interest Dangers

Clearly, all ISO 9001 quality assurance/management systems aren't equal, as all registrars and registrations aren't equal. Indeed, there are organizations that support both registrars and separate consulting divisions. Even though these two entities are separate legal corporations, a few operations have implied "one-stop shopping"— a conflict of interest and potential liability exposure. Such blurring of lines is a violation of the rules of the Registrar Accreditation Board (RAB) for QMS registrars.

It is important for attorneys to know that all quality systems are not equal and that, here and there, the line between consulting companies and registrars has been blurred. Many issues could affect your client and go to the heart of a lawsuit. These issues could range from conflict-of-interest to misleading a client to failure to warn a client of the results of a particular action, thereby causing injury to a client. Understanding the structure of ISO 9001 and the dynamics of the registration process could become a key to your client's legal interests.

> **Note**: To obtain copies of the ISO 9000 standards, contact one of the sources listed in Appendix E on page 179. For a brief review of the clauses in ISO 9001, see Appendix A on page 119.

Liability Exposure

> **Important:** In the event of a lawsuit, if a company has a registered ISO 9001-based QMS, the documentation can be obtained through discovery to determine whether the requirements under Clause 4.4, Design Control, have been satisfactorily addressed and audited. The key to any company's defense will be adequate and effective documentation.

Liability Exposure of Documentation

From the list of clauses and subclauses in Table 1-2 on page 17, it is clear that ISO 9001 registration can represent a significant accomplishment. Furthermore, it is a fully documented QA system that records work results demonstrating performance to documentation. ISO 9001 can be a powerful methodology that provides a paper trail documenting compliance with an effective quality system in the event of a lawsuit. Conversely, it also can represent a significant degree of exposure if the paper trail reveals a weak quality system that is not able to document all of the elements of a QMS or that documents failure to adhere to the QA system. The good news and the bad news are identical: a paper trail exists in the event of a lawsuit.

Liability Exposure of Professional Advice

All participants in the ISO 9000 quality assurance process are vulnerable to liability exposure. This includes the company itself, the consultants who help construct the quality system, the third-party registrar that audits the quality system and issues the certificate of registration and the auditors employed by the registrar. It would behoove all participants to examine their legal roles in the process.

For consultants, registrars and auditors, the quality of their professional advice, expertise and competence—or lack thereof—subjects them to the same liability for professional malpractice that affects the activities of doctors and lawyers. If a person or a company believes that financial and/or legal problems stem from bad advice or incompetence, it is the prerogative of the individual or company to use the courts to redress any grievances.

For example, a training program of a medical device manufacturer may be minimally acceptable under ISO 9001 Clause 4.18, Training even though the supplier has established and maintained documented procedures for identifying training needs and providing for the training of all personnel affecting quality. Yet, on examination it becomes apparent to the auditor that these personnel were not sufficiently trained to deal with the subtleties of differentiating between old and new models of a medical device, such as a dialysis machine.

Clearly, the auditor must have the ability to understand training as it relates to such devices and understand the appropriate level of education and training as it relates to these tasks. To lightly pass over a critical task by accepting a company's training as adequate might satisfy an auditor's accountability under an ISO 9000 standard, but it may not satisfy legal accountability in a court of law. In the best of all possible worlds, these two levels of accountability should be equal. However, if they are not, legal expectations for accountability will prevail in a court of law.

Consulting companies and registrars must realize that they, too, are vulnerable to liability lawsuits and constitute potential "deep pockets" for prospective plaintiffs. Consequently, they must take care to preserve their professional integrity and keep their liability exposure to a minimum. Already, various firms have cut corners in pursuit of clients, and some professional liability lawsuits are inevitable in the next few years.

Ignorance Is No Excuse

Consider one additional point—no quality system whatsoever! If a plaintiff's attorney were to pursue a defendant in a liability lawsuit and, in a deposition with a video camera, walk a defendant through all 20 clauses and the subclauses of ISO 9001 to compare and contrast ANSI/ASQ Q9001 (the US equivalent to ISO 9001) for a quality system with the defendant's absence of a quality system, the results could be profoundly embarrassing and potentially devastating. The negative image presented by demonstrating no quality control frequently has been so overwhelming that it has led to out-of-court settlements.

Lines of Questioning

The following study of several clauses and subclauses of ISO 9001 will demonstrate how ISO 9001 could be used to examine a weakly documented quality system or expose a lack thereof.

These lines of questioning will provide any company with the tools to follow Sun Tsu's offensive strategy axiom: "Know the enemy and know yourself; in a hundred battles you will never be in peril." The lines of questioning in this and subsequent chapters will allow a company to evaluate the weaknesses of its QMS from a legal perspective. The key to using these lines of questioning is to examine the QMS with them *before* legal battles arise.

4.4 Design Control

One area that causes difficulty is design. In fact, design is a major reason that the FDA has harmonized its recently released *Quality System Regulation* (QSR)—often referred to as the new GMPs—with the requirements of ISO 9001 (see page 108).

4.4.1 — General

The prescriptive language of the standard is especially helpful in articulating key questions and could be devastating to a non-ISO 9001-registered company. For example, the **General** subclause under design control states:

The supplier [i.e., company] *shall establish and maintain*

documented procedures to control and verify the design of the product in order to ensure that the specified requirements are met. [Emphasis added.]

Follow-Up Questions:

- What are your company's specified requirements?
- Why did your company choose these specifications?
- What procedures did your company establish to verify the design with these requirements?
- How are these documented?
- How is this documentation controlled?
- Are any of your company's design requirements not specified or documented?

4.4.2 — Design and Development Planning

The **Design and Development Planning** subclause states:

The supplier [i.e., company] *shall prepare plans for each design and development activity.* The plans *shall describe or reference these activities, and define responsibility* for their implementation. The design and development activities *shall be assigned to qualified personnel equipped with adequate resources.* The plans *shall be updated,* as the design evolves. [Emphasis added.]

Follow-Up Questions:

- Do you have plans for each design and development activity?
- What are these plans and how do they relate to each design and development activity?
- 4.4.2 states that these plans reference design and development activities and define implementation responsibilities. Can you identify these references and definitions?
- How are implementation responsibilities defined?
- Why are they defined in this manner?

- 4.4.2 states further that these design and development activities shall be assigned to qualified personnel. What are these qualifications and how were they determined?

- How did you identify and recruit selected personnel?

- Who are these personnel?

- Finally, this subclause states that resources are to be adequate and that plans be updated. What are the resources that have been allocated to these personnel to carry out their tasks?

- What are your plans for design updates?

- Have any designs been updated?

- Why and when were they updated?

4.9 Process Control

A similar breakdown could be made for production. Rather than examine the entire section, the initial paragraph helps to illustrate this clause, especially for a manufacturing operation:

> The supplier *shall identify and plan* the production, installation and servicing processes [that] affect quality and shall ensure that these processes are carried out under controlled conditions. Controlled conditions *shall include the following:*
>
> a) documented procedures defining the manner of production, installation and servicing, where the absence of such procedures could adversely affect quality;
>
> b) use of suitable production, installation and servicing equipment, and a suitable working environment;
>
> c) compliance with reference standards/codes, quality plans and/or documented procedures;
>
> d) monitoring and control of suitable process parameters and product characteristics;
>
> e) the approval of processes and equipment, as appropriate;
>
> f) *criteria for workmanship, which* shall be stipulated *in the clearest practical manner (e.g., written standards,*

representative samples or illustrations)…
[Emphasis added].

Follow-Up Questions:

- How does your company identify and plan the production, installation and servicing procedures that affect quality?

- What steps does your company take to assure quality in repetitive or *series* manufacture? *Note: "series manufacture" refers to production of everything but one-of-a-kind machines.*

- What steps does your company take to ensure that your manufacturing processes are carried out under controlled conditions?

- What sort of statistical techniques does your company use to establish, control and verify process capability and product characteristics?

- What are your company's documented procedures for defining the manner of production, installation and servicing? (This could be broken down into three questions.)

- What rationale does your company use to define suitable production, installation and servicing equipment?

- What procedures and/or standards does your company use to define a suitable working environment?

- How has your company complied with reference standards, industry standards, codes, quality plans and/or documented procedures?

- How does your company monitor and control suitable process parameters and how do you control product characteristics?

- How does your company approve processes and equipment?

- How does your company determine the criteria for workman-ship—by written standards, illustrations, representative samples?

- Does your company train people to meet these workmanship criteria? How? Does your company measure the effectiveness of your training?

4.16 Control of Quality Records

The following excerpts from this clause state:

- The supplier *shall establish* and maintain documented procedures

- Quality records *shall be maintained* to demonstrate conformance to specified requirements and the effective operation of the quality system

- All quality records *shall be legible and shall be stored and retained* in such a way that they are readily retrievable [Emphasis added.]

Follow-Up Questions:

- How does your company establish and maintain documented procedures for identifying training needs?

- What are those procedures?

- How does your company determine which personnel perform activities affecting quality?

- How does your company train these personnel?

4.18 Training

Clause 4.18 of ISO 9001 states:

The supplier *shall establish and maintain documented procedures* for identifying training needs and provide for the training of all personnel performing activities affecting quality. Personnel performing specific assigned tasks *shall be qualified on the basis of appropriate education, training* and/or experience, as required. Appropriate records *shall be* maintained. (see 4.16) [Emphasis added.]

Training offers a productive area for consideration in a lawsuit. The noble term "increased productivity" frequently masks savings derived from "dumbing down" personnel by hiring less expensive employees with minimal skills. While this practice might be offset by increasing skill levels through training, often this does not occur.

Attorneys already have discovered that poorly trained employees often lead to accidents such as the situation where a pedestrian was hit by tiles handled by an untrained employee. In the instances cited in a recent article, these cases have led to out-of-court settlements, rather than a trial (John R. Broomfield, "Lawyers Wise Up to ISO 9000", *Compliance Engineering*, Volume 13, Number 1).

Follow-Up Questions:

- How does your company establish what is appropriate education, training or experience for its personnel?

- What training does your company provide to achieve appropriate levels of education?

- What does your company consider to be appropriate records?

- What are those records?

- What are your company's documented procedures for training?

- What quality records does your company maintain to demonstrate conformance to specified requirements for effective operation of the quality system?

- How are these records stored?

Summary

Withstanding Legal Scrutiny

It should be apparent from the preceding clauses dealing with Design Control (General and Design and Development Planning), Process Control and Training (cross-referenced to Control of Quality Records) that detailed sets of questions can be developed for each and every clause and subclause of ISO 9001. If a company's quality management program is well-constructed and well-documented, it should be able to sustain the scrutiny of a legal challenge. It is quite clear, however, that the quality of documentation will be crucial.

If a company's quality system is weakly constructed and documented, it should anticipate that those weaknesses may be examined in-depth by the plaintiff's counsel to determine if those weaknesses offer useful vantage points to exploit in litigation; e.g., weak design, planning, purchasing, process control, inspection, control of nonconforming product, handling, quality records, training and servicing. Not all registered systems are equal and weak systems are vulnerable.

Liability Exposure of Documentation

ISO 9001 can be a powerful methodology that provides a paper trail documenting compliance with an effective quality system in the event of a lawsuit. Conversely, it also can represent a significant degree of exposure if the paper trail reveals a weak quality system that is not able to document all of the elements of a QMS or that documents failure to adhere to the QA system. The good news and the bad news are identical: a paper trail exists in the event of a lawsuit.

Liability Exposure of Professional Advice

All participants in the ISO 9000 quality assurance process are vulnerable to lability exposure. It would behoove all participants (i.e., the company obtaining registration, the ISO 9000 trainers and consultants, the registrar and its employees and auditors) to examine their legal roles in the process. If a person or company believes that financial problems stem from bad advice or incompetence, it is the prerogative of the person or company to use the courts to redress any grievances. For consultants, registrars and auditors, the quality of their professional advice, expertise and competence subjects them to the same liability for professional malpractice as doctors and lawyers.

Exclusion of Design Control

If a company is registered to ISO 9002 because it chose to exclude design control from the rigors and scrutiny of registration, it should anticipate potential legal challenges on this point. Whatever the reasons for avoiding scrutiny on design in ISO 9001, if design becomes an issue in litigation, companies should anticipate that their design records can be obtained in discovery. These records combined with pointed questions about design control—including design and development planning, organizational and technical interfaces, design input, design output, design review, design verification, design validation and design changes in ISO 9001—could prove awkward and possibly damaging to a legal defense. The implication is that design was excluded because it wasn't under control and incapable of withstanding the scrutiny of registration.

Companies With No QA System

Important: If the absence of a quality system exposes a company to liability lawsuits when its practices and behaviors are contrasted with the structured practices and behaviors of a registered quality system, then ISO 9001/2/3 registration soon may become the price of doing business in the United States. It will become a minimum hurdle for US businesses.

If a company has no registered and/or no internal QA system, it is vulnerable to a challenge on each and every clause and subclause of ISO 9001. On legal discovery, product liability attorneys easily can find out if a company observes the requirements of ANSI/ASQ Q9001 (i.e., ISO 9001). Already, plaintiffs' counsel have presented the following arguments in various cases:

- The absence of documented training and inspections has allowed flawed products to reach consumers, resulting in injuries.

- The lack of employee training in the handling of products resulted in injury to a bystander.

- The absence of a documented quality system allowed nonconforming product to reach a consumer, resulting in injury.

All of these cases were resolved out of court—with five- to six-figure settlements resulting.

ISO 9000 Expansion

Finally, attorneys should prepare for a veritable explosion of ISO 9001/2/3 registrations in the marketplace because of customer pressures (e.g., the automotive industry and QS-9000). In addition, another level of growth will be fueled by the use of ISO 9001/2/3 as a conformity assessment requirement in US- and EU-regulated industries.

Scenarios

Scenario 3

Supreme Machines, Inc., manufactures blow molding plastics machinery for the bottling industry. Well-respected in the United States, Supreme had been approached by several European customers wanting to purchase some of its most popular models. In most instances these EU customers stipulated that the machines must be CE-marked in accordance with all relevant EU Directives. A CE (*Conformité Européenne* in French or *European Conformity* in English) mark is a certification mark applied to a product, indicating that the product conforms to the requirements specified in an EU Directive. If a Directive applies to your company's product, a CE mark demonstrating your product's verified conformance to the Directive's specifications is a requirement to sell your product legally in the EU. CE-marking is a certification process provided by EU-notified bodies. However, a few EU customers did indicate that Supreme need not worry about CE-marking, that the customer would handle it on its end. Supreme learned that countries such a Spain, Germany, France, Sweden and the UK have become especially vigilant in impounding non-CE-marked machines at customs. Supreme even heard that one non-CE-marked machine that had been installed on a plant floor was discovered and ordered removed by UK authorities, imposing on the manufacturer a fine and a six-month suspended sentence under the criminal code.

To comply with the EU's Machinery, Electromagnetic Compatibility (EMC) and Low Voltage Directives, Supreme contracted with Dynamo Testing, Ltd., to certify Supreme's compliance with the requirements of the EMC and Low Voltage Directives and to CE-mark its machinery for both directives. With the help of a consultant, Supreme also began to construct technical files for self-certification of its more popular models to the Machinery Directive. As a first step, Supreme developed an Annex I - Essential

Safety Requirements checklist for each technical file. These check-lists identified the essential safety requirements that applied to the various product models. Following this step, Supreme identified the relevant EN (European Norm) safety standards that would allow it to demonstrate product safety conformity with the essential safety requirements for each of its models.

Fortunately for Supreme, there is a Type C Machine specific safety standard that will allow it to demonstrate conformity: *EN422;1995 Rubber and Plastics Machines-Safety—Blow Moulding Machines Intended for the Production of Hollow Articles-Requirements for the Design and Construction*. This standard, in turn, references the following standards:

- *EN292-1:1991, Safety of Machinery—Basic Concepts, General Principles for Design. Part 1: Basic Terminology and Methodology*

- *EN292-2:1991, Safety of Machinery—Basic Concepts, General Principles for Design. Part 2: Technical Principles and Specifications*

- *EN294:1992, Safety of Machinery—Safety Distances to Prevent Danger Zones from Reach by Upper Limbs*

- *EN414:1992, Safety of Machinery—Presentation of Safety Standards*

- *EN418:1992, Safety of Machinery—Emergency Stop Relevant Functional Aspects*

- *EN573, Safety of Machinery—Temperature of Touchable Surfaces, Ergonomic Data for the Provision of Limit Values for Hot Surfaces*

- *EN60204-1, Electrical Equipment of Industrial Machines—Part 1, General Requirements*

- *IEC 801-2, Electromagnetic Compatibility for Industrial Process Measurement and Control Equipment—Part 2, Electrostatic Discharge Requirements*

- *ISO 3744, Acoustics—Determination of Sound Power Levels of Noise Sources; Engineering Method Employing Measurement Surface in an Essentially Free Field over a Reflecting Plane.*

To this list it was necessary to add *EN1050, Safety of Machinery— Risk Assessment, Hazard Identification and Selection of Safety Measures.*

Because Supreme was able to self-certify to the Machinery Directive, it followed the instructions for constructing a technical file contained in Annex 5 of the Directive.

Included in the technical file are:

- An overall drawing of the machinery model together with drawings of the control circuits

- Full detailed drawings, accompanied by calculation notes, test results, etc., required to check the conformity of the machinery with the essential safety requirements (including the requirements of the various Blow Molding Plastics Machinery standards identified by Supreme)

- Essential safety requirements checklist

- The list of EN, ISO and IEC Safety Standards used to identify conformity with the essential safety requirements

- Other technical specifications used to design the machines

- A description of methods adopted by Supreme to eliminate safety hazards presented by the machines (in accordance with EN1050)

- Technical reports and certificates from Dynamo Testing, Ltd., indicating compliance with the requirements of the EMC and Low Voltage Directives

- A copy of instructions for the machinery

- A copy of the EC (European Community) Declaration of Conformity indicating compliance with the Machinery, EMC and Low Voltage Directives and relevant safety standards

- A copy of the quality manual and procedures for the quality system adopted by Supreme to assure consistent product quality in manufacture.

The Machinery Directive was developed before the EU adopted its modular approach utilizing the ISO 9000 series, allowing Supreme the option of listing its own internal quality system instead of an ISO 9001-based system. However, the company chose to register to ISO 9001 in response to market demands. Supreme indicated its registration to ISO 9001 on its Declaration of Conformity.

The Case

One year after Supreme began exporting its first CE-marked models to the EU market, an accident occurred in the US involving model SUPM-3. In this instance, the operator of the machine was using a two-hand control that effectively prevented operator access to moving parts of the blow molding machine. (If the operator removed one hand from the controls for the machine, it would automatically shut down.)

The accident occurred when a second person in charge of machine maintenance lifted a hinged guard in an effort to clear out excess scrap plastic by hand. As he was reaching in to clean the scrap plastic, the machine was preparing to slice away excess plastic from the mold, called the "guillotine phase". As a consequence, the guillotine blade severed the maintenance worker's hand.

The Attack and Defense

In the discovery phase for the client, the plaintiff's attorney learned that Supreme was producing two versions of the blow molding machine. The US version of the SUPM-3 did not have a safety interlock for the hinged guard, whereas the CE-marked version did have a safety interlock in compliance with the safety requirements of the Machinery Directive (the safety interlocks would have shut the machine down automatically if the maintenance worker had used a key to lift the hinged guard). Further, both machines had been manufactured at approximately the same time. Clearly, Supreme was manufacturing for two different markets since the CE-marked model contained safety features that were absent from the machines sold in the US market.

In addition, the plaintiff's attorney noted that both machines were manufactured in a plant registered to ISO 9001. Therefore, the attorney also alleged that Supreme was not consistent in establishing its design input requirements. ISO 9001 states in Clause 4.4, Design, Subclause 4.4.4, Design Input:

> Design-input requirements relating to the product, including applicable statutory and regulatory requirements, shall be identified, documented and their selection reviewed by the supplier for adequacy. Incomplete, ambiguous or conflicting requirements shall be resolved with those re-

sponsible for imposing these requirements.

Design input must take into consideration the results of any contract review activities.

Without directly saying so, design input also requires examination of safety considerations because it will affect design output, which is discussed below. In addition, EN46001 specifies that safety must be considered in design input relative to its impact on design output.

Further, the plaintiff's attorney found that in addition to meeting design-input requirements as stipulated in subparagraph (a) of Subclause 4.4.5, Design Output, subparagraph (c) states that design output shall:

> identify those characteristics of the design that are crucial to the safe and proper functioning of the product (e.g., operating, storage, handling, maintenance and disposal requirements).

The plaintiff's attorney noted that Supreme was fully aware that it could make a safer product, because it was already doing so to meet CE-marking requirements in the EU. The attorney argued that Supreme should have imposed those same safety requirements for its US products, in accordance with Subclauses 4.4.4, Design Input and 4.4.5, Design Output.

Further, the plaintiff's attorney argued that Supreme should have reviewed ISO 9004-1 in constructing its ISO 9001 quality system. In particular, Supreme should have reviewed Subclause 8.2.4 of Clause 8.2, Design Planning and Objectives, which states:

> In addition to customer needs, consideration should be given to the requirements relating to safety, environmental, and other regulations, including items in the organization's quality policy which may go beyond existing statutory requirements (see also 3.3).

The attorney also argued that Supreme should have considered Subclause 8.4.2, Elements of Design Reviews, regarding items pertaining to customer needs and satisfaction, including: "4) unintended uses and misuses; and 6) compliance with regulatory requirements, national and International Standards, and organization practices." The plaintiff's attorney concluded by noting that Supreme also could not provide evidence to document its review of ISO 9004-1, Section 19, Product Safety.

Supreme's defense counsel was appalled at its position and was frustrated by the lack of input by Supreme's in-house corporate counsel during the design phases of product development. Further, it was clear on a review of ISO 9001 that corporate counsel was not consulted in conformance to the requirements of Subclause 4.4.3, Organizational and Technical Interfaces. Had this been done and had Supreme's design personnel revealed that the company was going to manufacture two different versions of the same model SUPM-3 for two markets—one at a higher safety level than the other—in-house counsel could have objected. Clearly, a substantial liability was created by the manufacture of safer and less safe versions of the same model. Supreme should have opted to make only the safer CE-marked version for both markets.

While it was apparent that the most likely and least damaging resolution of this accident was to settle with the plaintiff out of court, both Supreme's defense and in-house counsel learned some valuable lessons for future designs. First, it is critical that attorneys be included in the loop to participate in relevant phases of the design process, not to prevent products from coming to market, but to understand and participate in the process. Second, it is clear that attorneys need to better understand the workings of the CE-marking process and how it impacts liability exposure for the domestic market as well as the EU and global markets. Third, had the Machinery Directive technical file for model SUPM-3 contained key safety standards information for the US market as it did for the EU market, it could have provided an excellent vehicle for a legal defense in the event of a lawsuit, because it contained documentation of Supreme' attention to product safety.

Conclusions

As noted in the previous two scenarios, no one yet knows how a judge or jury might respond to the line of attack proposed by the plaintiff's counsel. However, cases that have exposed practices such as making the same product at two different levels of safety generally have been decided for the plaintiff. Clearly, the defendant knew how to make a safer machine and did so for Europe, but not for the US.

It is important to understand the use of an ISO 9001-based quality management system in a regulated environment. In this scenario, the EU has created a set of Directives (laws) with which any firm intending to "place its products on the EU market" must comply. CE-marking is an EU legal requirement for products governed by EU new approach directives.

Most EU Directives contain two dimensions:

1) The creation of a technical file that identifies a directive's "essential safety requirements" and the safety standing that allows a company to demonstrate conformity with those essential requirements.

2) The creation of a quality system (conformity assessment procedure) that demonstrates how a company will maintain consistent quality in manufacturing a safe product.

Because this EU approach is gaining global acceptance and is being adopted by non-EU countries and multinational corporations based in Australia, Brazil, India, Japan, the US, etc., as a contract requirement, CE-marking has directly and indirectly entered the US marketplace.

In the manufacture of medical devices, the EU and FDA have harmonized their approaches to product safety and quality system management. Consequently, attorneys will need to understand the legal implications of the interplay between these two dimensions.

Attorneys should expect that these models will continue to grow and evolve in the future—mixing requirements for product safety (e.g., a technical file) with quality system requirements for consistent quality in the manufacture of safe products.

Chapter III

Quality Systems and Product Safety

OVERVIEW

This chapter focuses on the use of documentation to demonstrate systematic attention to the product and to product safety, from inception and design to production, monitoring and feedback. In order to enforce the importance of documentation, excerpts from ISO 9004-1 (a guidance document that should be studied by any company considering registration to ISO 9001/2/3) are broken down clause by clause with a series of questions that could be used by a company to examine its use of this QMS guidance standard.

KEY POINTS

❖ It is possible for a first-rate quality system to make a mediocre product extremely well if the focus is on the system, not the product.

❖ ISO 9001/2/3 registration cannot of itself reduce liability exposure of a company. Only systematic affirmative steps to address product safety issues will impress a court of law.

❖ A fully documented ISO 9001/2/3 registered quality assurance system may even increase liability exposure if it documents inattention to product safety issues.

❖ A commitment to product safety will require more than meeting minimum government standards.

❖ In the US, guidance documents that are a part of a series (like ISO 9004-1) help to establish a manufacturer's "duty of care" and can be used by courts to establish evidence of negligence or evidence of a design defect.

❖ Both plaintiff and defense attorneys should consider seeking assistance when interpreting ISO 9001 and ISO 9004-1. Be certain to find someone conversant with ISO 9004-1 and capable of providing constructive assistance, rather than someone convinced that it is not a conformance standard and therefore irrelevant.

Focus on the Product

One oft-cited shortcoming of the ISO 9000 conformance standards is that a first-rate quality assurance system could make a mediocre product extremely well, because the focus is on the system, not the product. While the frequently repeated statement that "an ISO 9001/2/3 registered quality system could make a concrete life jacket" is an overstatement and not entirely accurate, it does help to emphasize the QA system/product dichotomy.

ISO 9000 Registration Is Not Enough

Another aspect of ISO 9000 registration is the often espoused but unproven axiom that "ISO 9000 is a great defense in the event of a product liability lawsuit!" This notion was fed enthusiastically to prospective clients by various ISO 9000 consulting firms as early as 1990. It picked up additional steam when some UK insurance companies offered 20 to 40 percent discounts to companies registered to ISO 9001/2/3.

While the offer never crossed the Atlantic to the US and was confined to operations in the UK and Europe, the liability-reducing virtues of ISO 9001/2/3 registration were touted to prospective US clients by US consultants nonetheless. It was a foolish boast that could come back to haunt these same consultants if an injured company were able to employ a legal doctrine such as "reliance" to sue a firm that made such a statement (e.g., "We pursued ISO 9001/2/3 registration specifically because we relied on ISO 9000 Consulting Company X's claim that it would reduce our liability exposure, but in fact it increased our exposure!").

As noted in Chapter I, the good news about ISO 9001/2/3 registration is that a company now has a paper trail in the event of a lawsuit...and the bad news is that the same company now has a paper trail in the event of a lawsuit. The quality of the company's paper trail is what will determine whether ISO 9001/2/3 registration will be helpful or harmful to that company.

Product Safety

The critical issue for a legal defense in most jurisdictions will revolve around the issue of product safety. This includes the ability of a company to demonstrate and document:

- Its commitment to product safety

- Its production of safe products from design through manufacturing

- Its provision of appropriate warnings and instructions to customers at purchase

- Its fulfillment of all postsale obligations

- Its maintenance of postsale monitoring.

If the paper trail reveals that little or no attention has been paid to product safety, the company's ISO 9001/2/3-registered QA system will have documented the company's indifference and/or inattention to issues of product safety. The company also will have increased its liability exposure.

On the other hand, if the paper trail reveals that product safety was a company value and the company took specific steps to increase product safety, the company's ISO 9001/2/3 documentation could be a valuable asset in a product liability lawsuit. As noted earlier, it depends on the quality of the paper trail as a legal defense in a court of law!

Naturally the issue of product safety is calibrated to the degree of safety risk presented by the product. High-risk products such as heart pacemakers, electric saws and toxic chemicals will require a greater number of safety steps and closer scrutiny than low-risk products such as tennis balls, paint brushes and tongue depressors.

In all likelihood, high-risk products also will have to meet minimum safety regulations in the US, EU, Japan, Canada and other jurisdictions. For example, products such as implantable medical devices are highly regulated in all nations. Market entry will require some form of prior government approval before being offered for sale to the public.

Avoid Bare Minimum Compliance

A commitment to product safety, however, will require more than meeting minimum government standards. Courts will be evaluating many factors, including:

- The existence of a company safety policy and its dissemination to and comprehension by employees

- The assignment of safety responsibilities to more than a single individual (e.g., a product safety committee)

- A visible commitment by executive management to product safety (e.g., line responsibility to a vice president who reports to the president).

Courts also will be looking for evidence of a concern for product safety in product design, the safe use of product software and risk assessment, which might incorporate steps such as Hazard Analysis, Failure Modes and Effects Analysis (FMEA), Fault Tree Analysis (FTA) or Operational Hazard Analysis (HAZOP). To this list should be added various aspects of product presentation (e.g., warnings and instructions, postsale monitoring, ergonomic considerations, human factors analysis) and calculations of foreseeable use and foreseeable misuse.

Product Safety Documentation Is Key

Whatever the elements of the approach, a company will impress a court of law if it displays the systematic attention to product safety from inception and design through to production, monitoring and feedback. Consequently, it will be systematic attention to product safety, referenced and documented within an ISO 9001/2/3-based quality assurance system, that will provide a persuasive defense in a product liability lawsuit.

Therefore, if a company wishes to incorporate its ISO 9001/2/3-registered quality assurance system into a liability defense program—also called a preventive law program—it will be necessary to take systematic affirmative steps to address product safety issues.

Further, these steps will need to be identified and documented as an element of an ISO 9001/2/3-based quality assurance system in order to be used as a defense in a prospective lawsuit. These issues are discussed in Chapter IV, Beyond ISO 9000… A Preventive Program.

ISO 9001/2/3 and Product Safety

Very little specific language exists in the three conformance standards (ISO 9001, ISO 9002 and ISO 9003) that focuses on the issue of product safety. While it might be argued that safety should be an implicit requirement, courts will look for explicit evidence of that commitment. The most obvious statement can be found in ISO 9001, 4.4.5, Design Control—Design Output:

> c) identify those characteristics of the design that are crucial to the safe and proper functioning of the product (e.g., operating, storage, handling, maintenance and disposal requirements).

Since this is a component of design output, Design Input (Subclause 4.4.4) could be added through the language in Design Verification (4.4.7):

> At appropriate stages of design, design verification shall be performed to ensure that the design stage output meets the design stage input requirements.

Several US attorneys have indicated that Clause 4.4, Design Control in ISO 9001 would provide the legal entry point to evaluate the substance of a company's concern for product safety. Does this mean that companies registering to ISO 9002 or ISO 9003 don't have to respond? Of course not. As noted earlier, someone is responsible for the safe design of a product and is liable if the product's unsafe design were to cause injury.

It does mean, however, that companies registering to ISO 9001 should give design output careful consideration. While Subclause 4.2.3, Quality Planning, does mention design compatibility and *capability that exceeds the known state of the art,* the reference is a bit too oblique to make it central to a product liability lawsuit.

ISO 9004-1 and Product Safety

In the US, guidance documents such as ISO 9000-1 and ISO 9004-1 are considered components of the series along with ISO 9001, ISO 9002 and ISO 9003. *ISO 9000-1, Quality Management and Quality Assurance Standards—Guidelines for Selection and Use* is a useful "road map" that acquaints companies with the ISO 9000 series, explains fundamental quality concepts and helps companies select, use and tailor ISO 9001/2/3 to meet their quality assurance needs. As has already been discussed, ISO 9004-1's role is to guide a company in establishing an effective QMS. As such, even though these are guidance standards, they can be used to examine issues such as product safety. Further, these guidance standards ask questions that every company should ask itself when establishing a quality assurance system.

Duty of Care

In the US, guidance documents that are a part of a series help to establish a manufacturer's "duty of care" and can be used by courts to establish evidence of negligence or of a design defect. A plaintiff's attorney could argue that the issues raised by ISO 9004-1 should be considered first by any responsible company before registering to any other standard in the series.

The ISO 9000 Paper Trail

Product Safety Liability Exposure

A cursory review of the outline of ISO 9004-1 provided in Table 1-1 on pages 15-16 gives an indication of the substantive detail contained within this guidance standard. Logically, a company should first review and discuss the relevant clauses of ISO 9004-1 before developing its strategy for an ISO 9001/2-based quality management program.

Unfortunately, this is rarely the case. Most companies focus on their chosen conformance standard without giving consideration to the issues raised by ISO 9004-1. It is a shortsighted mistake with potentially significant legal consequences.

The following discussion of excerpts from ISO 9004-1 "requirements" indicates a range of questions that its recommendations raise, which could have an impact upon product safety and underline where an absence of response to product safety could create product liability exposures.

Product Safety Focus in ISO 9004-1

3.3 Requirements of Society

Obligations resulting from laws, regulations, rules, codes, statutes, and other considerations.

[This includes] protection of the environment, health, safety, security, and conservation of energy and natural resources.

Follow-Up Questions:

• What steps did your company take to determine which laws, regulations, rules, codes and statutes affected its operations?

• In considering your company's products, what steps has it taken to deal with protection of the environment? (This question would be better addressed with the environmental management system standards *ISO 14001, Environmental Management Systems—Specification with Guidance for Use* and *ISO 14004, Environmental Management System—General Guidelines on Principles, Systems and Supporting Techniques.*)

5 Quality-System Elements
5.1 Extent of Application

Subclause 5.1.1 involves:

all phases in the life cycle of a product or processes...[Typical phases are:]

g) packaging and storage;

k) after sales;

l) disposal or recycling at the end of useful life.

Follow-Up Questions:

• What efforts has your company made to determine the life cycle(s) of your product(s) and processes?

• What steps has your company taken to identify the impact of packaging and storage on the life cycle(s) of your product(s)?

• What is the expected life cycle(s) of your product(s) after sale?

• How has your company instructed consumers to deal with disposal of your product(s) after its useful life?

5.2.2 Responsibility and Authority

a) General and specific quality-related responsibilities should be explicitly defined.

Follow-Up Questions:

- Please provide explicit definitions for those positions that involve responsibility for quality in your company.

- To whom do these employees report? Do they have line authority or do they hold staff positions? *Note: In this case, persons holding staff positions report to another, while persons having line authority have direct budget responsibility.*

5.2.6 Configuration Management

This discipline is initiated early in the design phase and continues through the whole life cycle of a product.

Follow-Up Questions:

- How is quality in the design phase handled by your company?

- What are your documented procedures for configuration management from the design of a product throughout the product's life cycle? For example, what steps have been taken to relate product design to operation and control of design, production, product use and probable product lifetime? What steps were taken to deal with product safety at each of these stages?

5.3.2 Quality-System Documentation, 5.3.3 Quality Plans and 5.3.4 Quality Records

Your company's documentation, written to satisfy these elements, should reference the factors of product safety.

Follow-Up Questions:

- What steps has your company taken to document its quality system?

- How are your quality plans documented and maintained?

- What are those quality plans?

- What are your company's quality records for design, inspection, testing, surveys and audits?

- What has your company done to specifically identify efforts to improve product safety in its quality records?

6.2 Approaches to Financial Reporting of Quality-System Activities
6.2.2 (a) Quality-Costing Approach

[Includes the components of the costs for]

4) external failure: costs resulting from a product failing to meet the quality requirements after delivery (e.g., product maintenance and repair, warranties and returns, direct costs and allowances, product recall costs, liability costs).

_____

Follow-Up Question:

- What efforts has your company made to measure the costs of product maintenance, warranties and returns, product recalls and liabilities? If no efforts and measurements have been made, why not?

7.3 Customer Feedback Information

The marketing function should establish an information-monitoring and feedback system on a continuous basis.

_____

Follow-Up Questions:

- What can your company describe about its customer feedback system?

- How is your company utilizing product feedback information to design new products?

- How is your company utilizing product feedback information to update its information on product use and misuse?

8.2 Design Planning and Objectives (Defining the Project)

8.2.4 In addition to customer needs, consideration should

be given to the requirements relating to safety, environmental, and other regulations, including items in the organization's quality policy which may go beyond existing statutory requirements (see also 3.3).

Follow-Up Questions:

- What can your company tell the court about its designers' activities in terms of "safety, environmental, and other regulations, including items in the organization's quality policy which may go beyond existing statutory requirements?" If it cannot, why not?

- Does your company follow any industry standards? If yes, what are those standards?

8.2.5 Both fitness for purpose and safeguards against misuse should be considered. Product definition can also include dependability and serviceability through a reasonable life expectancy, including benign failure and safe disposability, as appropriate.

Follow-Up Questions:

- What has your company done about "fitness for purpose and safeguards against misuse"?

- How has your company defined product dependability and serviceability throughout a reasonable life expectancy, including benign failure and safe disposability?

8.4.2 Elements of Design Reviews

a) Items pertaining to customer needs and satisfaction

4) unintended uses and misuses;

6) compliance with regulatory requirements, national and International Standards, and organization practices;

b) Items pertaining to product specification

5) benign failure and fail-safe characteristics;

9) labeling, warnings, identification, traceability requirements, and user instructions

Follow-Up Questions:

- What has your company done to identify intended product uses and misuses?

- How has your company dealt with regulatory requirements as well as national and international standards?

- Does your company presently CE-mark or plan to CE-mark products for sale in the EU? If yes, under what directives does your company presently or plan to CE-mark?

- What steps has your company taken to identify and respond to benign failure and fail-safe characteristics?

- What has your company done for "labeling, warnings identification, traceability requirements, and user instructions"?

8.5 Design Qualification and Validation

The design process should provide periodic evaluation of the design at significant stages. Such evaluation can take the form of analytical methods, such as FMEA (failure mode and effect analysis), fault tree analysis, or risk assessment, as well as inspection and test of prototype models and/or actual product samples

Follow-Up Questions:

- Does your company use FMEAs, FTA or HAZOP analysis?

- What type of risk assessment does your company conduct during the product design process?

- Does your company inspect and test prototype models and/or product samples during your company's product design process?

- What steps does your company take to guard against hazards that can't be designed out?

11.2.2 Traceability

[E]nsure traceability to original material identification and verification status.

Follow-Up Questions:

● What steps does your company take to trace products or product batches throughout the production process from receipt of materials to delivery and installation of final product?

● If a product failed, how would your company trace the original product materials?

15.5 Analysis of Problem

[R]equiring careful analysis of the product specifications and of all related processes, operations, quality records, servicing reports, and customer complaints.

Follow-Up Question:

● Using your company's documentation system and procedures, how would it conduct a root cause analysis?

16.6 Market Feedback

A feedback system regarding performance in use should exist to monitor the quality characteristics of products throughout the life cycle.

Follow-Up Questions:

● How does your company's market feedback system "monitor the quality of products throughout the life cycle"? If it does not, why not?

● What measures does your company use to see if its product(s) satisfy customer expectations with regard to quality, safety and dependability?

19 Product Safety

Consideration should be given to identifying safety aspects of products and processes with the aim of enhancing safety. Steps can include:

a) identifying relevant safety standards in order to make the formulation of product specifications more effective;

b) carrying out design evaluation tests and prototype (or model) testing for safety and documenting the test results;

c) analyzing instructions and warnings to the user, maintenance manuals, and labeling and promotional material in order to minimize misinterpretation, particularly regarding intended use and known hazards;

d) developing a means of traceability to facilitate product recall (see 11.2, 14.2 and 14.6);

(e) considering development of an emergency plan in case recall of a product becomes necessary.

Follow-Up Questions:

- What steps does your company take to identify "safety aspects of products and processes with the aim of enhancing safety"?

- How does your company use safety standards to make product specifications more effective?

- What are those safety standards?

- Is your company aware of other safety standards in its industry and at the national and international levels? What is considered to be "state-of-the-art" safety in your industry?

- What design evaluation tests and prototype (or model) testing does your company conduct?

- How does this testing program relate to risk assessment during a product's design phase?

- How are these test results documented?

- What strategies does your company use to develop warnings and instructions for potential users?

- What efforts are made to address safety issues in maintenance manuals?

- What efforts are made to address safety issues in promotional materials to minimize misinterpretations?

- How does your company convey safety messages regarding intended use and known hazards?

- What efforts are made to direct labels, warnings and instructions to the educational level of intended, known and potential product users?

- What means has your company developed for product traceability in the event of a product recall?

- What emergency plans have been developed in case a product recall became necessary?

- What funds have been identified to fund the emergency plan, should it become necessary?

20 Use of Statistical Methods, 20.1 Applications

h) safety evaluation and risk analysis.

Follow-Up Question:

- How does your company use statistical methods for safety evaluation and risk analysis?

Summary

Focus on the Product

The ISO 9000 conformance standards (ISO 9001, ISO 9002 and ISO 9003) focus on the integrity of the QMS, not the product or service being provided by the quality management aspects of the system. It is possible for a strong quality system to effectively, efficiently and consistently manufacture a mediocre and, in some instances, poor product.

Demonstrating Product Safety Consciousness

The critical issue in a product liability lawsuit generally revolves around the issue of product safety and the ability of a company to demonstrate and document its commitment to product safety. If the ISO 9001/2/3 paper trail reveals that little or no attention has been paid to product safety, a company's ISO 9001/2/3 certificate of registration will have documented its indifference and/or inattention to product safety and will have increased the company's liability exposure.

ISO 9001/2/3 registration is not a great defense in the event of a lawsuit unless a company takes specific proactive efforts to document a demonstrated commitment to product (or service) safety. It will not happen as a simple matter of QA system registration!

Insurance companies that offer discounts in liability coverage without requiring that their insureds demonstrate a proactive commitment to product safety in their ISO 9001/2/3-based QMSs are courting disaster. On the other hand, insurance companies that ask for a proactive commitment by their insureds to product safety by recording systematic affirmative steps that address product safety issues in their ISO 9001/2/3-based QMSs should consider reducing liability premiums as a reward for reduced liability exposure.

Duty of Care

In the US, guidance documents such as ISO 9004-1 that are a part of a series (in this case the ISO 9000 QMS series) help to establish a manufacturer's "duty of care." Failure to examine ISO 9004-1 can be used by plaintiff's counsel to establish evidence of negligence and/or a design defect. More to the point, while ISO 9004-1 was designed to provide guidance on establishment of a QMS, it provides effective guidance for the three ISO 9000 conformance standards (ISO 9001, ISO 9002 and ISO 9003). As indicated in this chapter, plaintiff's counsel could argue that ISO 9004-1 raises critical questions and addresses issues that should be considered first by a responsible company before registering to any of these conformance standards.

Shoring Up Weaknesses

ISO 9004-1 amplifies every clause of ISO 9001. For liability purposes, companies should be able to answer each of the points in ISO 9004-1 as they relate to their ISO 9001-based QMS. A company must be capable of answering the various questions raised by any relevant clauses and indicate how this was handled by its ISO 9001/2-registered QMS.

Chapter IV

Beyond ISO 9001/2/3...
A Preventive Program

OVERVIEW

From Chapter III, it is easy to see how ISO 9004-1 can be used to develop questions to expand upon various aspects of ISO 9000-based quality management systems, especially the safety of products manufactured under those systems. Because a company in litigation should anticipate being questioned on both ISO 9001 and ISO 9004-1, it is important to examine each clause, determine which are relevant and decide how these clauses should be addressed when preparing for registration.

Being able to respond to applicable clauses, however, does not create a preventive law program. Accomplishing this objective may require going beyond the issues raised by ISO 9004-1 and addressing a series of legal concerns in a more systematic and comprehensive framework. This chapter identifies such a framework.

KEY POINTS

❖ Critical to the defense of a company in a product liability lawsuit will be its system for records management and documentation.

❖ Poor documentation or no documentation can be devastating in punitive jury awards when it is perceived that the company doesn't care about safety.

❖ Product design must prove that safety was a key concern in creating the product.

❖ It is vital that software producers and users understand the degree of safety required and carefully document their design efforts.

❖ Warnings and instructions are critical to product safety. Products have been found to be defective and manufacturers have been held liable when warnings and instructions are insufficient or absent.

❖ When providing product warranties and/or guarantees, competent legal advisors should closely review any contractual obligations for direct and implied legal commitments.

❖ All complaints must be given serious attention. It is legally unwise to turn customer service over to inept personnel whose behavior may provoke a lawsuit.

❖ Recalls provide a critical element in a product liability control program to demonstrate responsible behavior and a commitment to product safety.

❖ Approximately 35 percent of all product liability lawsuits involve component parts.

❖ Suppliers of basic components can be implicated in device liability lawsuits, so tolerances and operating limits must be clearly identified.

❖ Device manufacturers are responsible for the quality and safety of components introduced into their devices.

Building the Framework of a Preventive Law Program

Building a framework for an effective preventive law program would include elements such as:

- Records management and documentation
- Product design, including risk assessment and risk management
- Product design and software (where relevant)
- Warnings and instructions
- Postsale obligations
- Component parts.

While this list is not exhaustive and could be expanded and amplified to address the unique characteristics of various products, it does identify basic elements that should be given more systematic attention. This approach could be integrated with the various clauses of ISO 9004-1 and an ISO 9001 quality management program.

Records Management and Documentation

Critical to the defense of a company in a product liability lawsuit will be its system for records management and documentation. If you can't prove it, it doesn't exist!

ISO 9001 documentation is focused on the existence of a company quality manual for each plant, operating procedures, work instructions, company-specific records (forms, technical data, change orders) and document control. For purposes of sustaining a legal defense, it will be necessary to:

- Maintain and retain records (records disposal should occur only within a structured documents retention program)
- Include production methods
- Identify standards used to produce products, including qualitative and technical requirements
- Retain all marketing information (including instructions, catalogs, maintenance manuals and brochures)
- Identify any specific warnings and instructions (including

those required by the US Consumer Products Safety Commission, EPA, OSHA, FDA and those recommended by ANSI, ASTM, etc.)

● Identify any records of monitoring, customer feedback, complaints, etc.

In addition, companies should have policies in place that demonstrate a commitment to product safety, including:

● A coherent written safety policy that is distributed to and understood by company personnel.

● A policy that indicates that safety is a corporate objective.

● Safety responsibilities should be assigned to appropriate personnel.

● Top management should take an active role in the safety process.

● A policy that identifies specific personnel responsible for safety, methods for accountability, employee training, use of feedback, etc.

● A safety policy that indicates that the company follows safety standards, conducts safety reviews, uses systematic risk assessment, etc.

● Product design should be documented.

Companies should know that documents can be obtained through discovery, therefore:

● Assume anything written on paper or recorded on the computer (including e-mail) will last forever.

● Attempt to work on word control to avoid extravagant statements, inflammatory statements, humor, etc.

● Copy the minimum number of persons necessary following a company documentation policy.

● Keep communications moderate, open and candid.

● Don't speculate, exaggerate, assume facts not grounded on observation, etc.

● Close all information loops (questions should be answered).

● Know that "CYA" memos will draw attention.

The list could be expanded, but the point is made. What you

record can and will be used in a court of law. Documentation is a two-edged sword; it is critical to prove that a company is safety conscious, has a safety policy and is attempting to make safe products. However, poor documentation or no documentation can be devastating in punitive jury awards when it is perceived that the company doesn't care about safety.

Product Design, Including Risk Assessment/Management

Product design must prove that safety was a key concern in creating the product. To accomplish this objective, it is necessary to follow the basic safety hierarchy—what the Europeans call the principles of safety integration. Dangers should be:

● Designed out

● Guarded against if they can't be designed out

● Warned against if the first two options are not possible.

It should always be remembered, however, that great warnings do not compensate for a bad design! In various areas, the process of risk analysis can be aided by new standards for risk assessment. The Europeans have developed a risk assessment standard for machinery, EN (European Norm) 1050 and a risk assessment standard for medical devices, prEN (preliminary European Norm) 1441.

In turn, various European medical device standards are now under consideration by ISO Technical Committee 210 to create international standards for medical devices. TC 210 has already completed work on ISO 13485 and ISO 13488, which are applications of ISO 9001 and ISO 9002 to meet the needs of the medical device sector. The International Electrotechnical Commission (IEC) also has created two risk assessment/risk management standards for medical electrical devices. In the US, the Semiconductor Equipment and Materials International Association has developed a new "Safety Guideline for Risk Assessment".

Risk Assessment Concerns

What this means is that risk assessment options are being developed or may exist for many companies. It would be folly to ignore these options, guidelines, standards, etc., when creating a new product if safety is a concern. Types of questions that are asked in risk assessment include:

- Does the product present a risk of physical injury or damage to property if used as intended?

- If the product presents a risk, what is the risk? Can it be quantified in economic and social costs? (Identify and quantify each, if more than one risk exists.)

- Does the product pose a risk of injury or property damage if misused? Can the potential misuse be designed out, guarded against or warned against?

- Does the product present other foreseeable uses and misuses? Can these misuses be designed out, warned against or guarded against?

- Has the product been evaluated for potential product misuse, abuse or modification? Attach a value to the economic and social costs of misuse, abuse and modification.

- How does each new product your company develops compare with similar products for accidents, incidents, government regulatory actions, lawsuits, etc.?

- What are the factors influencing risk, such as the severity (degree of possible harm), frequency and duration of exposure, probability of occurrence and technical and human possibilities to permit avoidance of risk or harm?

- What are the human factors for risk, such as interaction with the product (machine, device, etc.), ergonomic effects, psychological aspects, training and experience?

- What is state-of-the-art with regard to this product?

- If this product is new, are there some comparisons available with similar product systems, from trade information and/or from use of components?

- Do lower risk alternatives exist that are feasible and similar in cost?

Risk Management Methodologies

In addition to the preceding risk assessment questions, methodologies exist for estimating factors influencing risks. Among these methodologies are:

Preliminary Hazard Analysis (PHA)

PHA is an inductive method that identifies hazardous situations and events that can cause harm for a specified system/subsystem component for all of its phases.

What-If Method

The What-If Method is used for uncomplicated applications. The method involves reviewing the process from raw materials to final product and formulating "what-if" questions and answers to evaluate the effects of component failures or procedural errors on the process.

Failure Mode and Effects Analysis (FMEA)

FMEA is an inductive method where the purpose is to evaluate the frequency and consequences of component failure. (It is not as useful for operating procedures and operator error.)

DEFI-METHOD

The DEFI-METHOD injects fault into a computerized system to determine the rate of failure to danger.

Fault Tree Analysis (FTA)

FTA is primarily a means of analyzing hazards that already have been identified using top-event frequency calculations.

DELPHI-TECHNIQUE

DELPHI-TECHNIQUE questions a large group of experts through a series of steps concentrating on those aspects for which no agreement has been reached. It is a forecasting method.

Hazard and Operability Study (HAZOP)

HAZOP is a systematic technique for identifying hazards and operability of a whole plant.

MOSCAR (Method Organized for a Systemic Analysis of Risks)

The MOSCAR Method is a complete approach, utilizing 10 steps, that analyzes the system and interacting subsystems from design to process to installation/use.

Finally, in addition to risk assessment questions and risk assessment methodologies, there are questions that should be asked of design systems. These questions should be folded into Clause 4.4, Design Control in ISO 9001 and Sections 8, Quality in Specification and Design, and 19, Product Safety, in ISO 9004-1. Among the items that should be considered are:

Technical Qualifications of Design Personnel

- Is product safety the responsibility of a single individual (e.g., product safety engineer) or is it the responsibility of a safety committee with key persons from R&D, engineering and design management, quality control, quality and executive management, regulatory, legal staff, insurance, etc.?

- If there is a product safety committee, does it participate in the design process? Can it ask for design and safety reviews, suggest modifications, stop production, etc.? Is the committee part of a feedback loop?

- If design changes are made, is there adequate documentation to assess these changes and identify how product safety entered into the decision making process?

- Are product designs subject to internal safety reviews? Are these reviews documented?

- Has purchasing done a safety review or analysis of raw materials, components and bought-in parts?

- If a design change affects product safety, is there a procedure for reengineering or retrofitting existing products?

- Is there full documentation of the use of safety integration principles by: designing out hazards; guarding against those hazards that can't be designed out; and warning against those hazards that can be neither designed out nor guarded against?

● Has full consideration been given to legal requirements for labels, warnings and instructions?

Product Design and Product Software

Increasingly, product software is becoming a product component, often in roles critical to safety. Because systematic failures can escape conventional test requirements and procedures, some risk management standards are being developed to test processes by which equipment is developed.

One such standard is the International Electrotechnical Commission's (IEC) *IEC 604-1-4: Medical Electrical Equipment— Part 1: General Requirements for Safety; 4: Collateral Standard: Safety Requirements for Programmable Electronic Medical Systems.* The Introduction to IEC 604-1-4 notes, "Pass/Fail criteria are, by themselves, inadequate to address the *safety of complex equipment.*"

For liability purposes, software design must be given specific attention since software failure can cause everything from the benign shutdown of a microwave oven to the failure of a critical life support medical device. Already, software failure is the subject of product liability lawsuits that can be expected to increase in number in the future.

For example, an employee of a plastics manufacturer got his arm caught in an auger that grinds used plastic for recycling. He sued the company, stating that the software didn't operate to stop the machine. Since the company was not able to identify what software had been sold with the machine, and could not disprove the claim, the case was settled out of court.

Because of the risks involved in the use of software for system control or hardware control, government agencies such as the Health and Safety Executive (HSE) in the United Kingdom have developed some guidance materials for "Programmable Electronic Systems." As noted by the HSE in *The Health and Safety Executive re Software*, "Virtually all programmable systems will, for the foreseeable future, include software in which the existence of errors is possible."

As a consequence, software producers and users must be diligent in evaluating safety risks. The higher the safety risk presented by a product, the greater the scrutiny must be when producing software. It is vital that software producers and users understand the degree of safety required and carefully document their design efforts.

HSE and IEC Software Criteria

A brief examination of some of the HSE and IEC software criteria is instructive.

HSE Software Criteria

First, the HSE identifies three system attributes that must be considered when creating software:

- Hardware reliability
- System configurations
- Overall quality.

HSE identifies the following steps for software producers and specifiers:

- Hazard analysis
- Risk assessment
- Analysis of system requirements—What are the systems requirements, the role of software in the system and the degree to which system safety depends on software?
  - What are the system safety requirements?
  - What regulatory requirements might affect software creation and operations (e.g., FDA, EPA, EU new approach safety directives or standards, industry standards)?
  - What are the software requirements and their operating limits?
  - What is the software design process?
  - What are the software review and test procedures?
  - What are the software systems tests?
  - What is the system's acceptance?

○ What are the maintenance requirements?

○ What are the feedback requirements and procedures?

At each stage of the preceding list, HSE requires that the following three elements must be reviewed.

Verification—At each stage of software development, the product must be tested and verified to make certain that it meets the requirements specified by the preceding stage.

Validation—At each stage, the system must be tested and evaluated to assure that the system meets the end user's requirements. Will the system accomplish its stated objectives?

Documentation—In addition to an overall safety quality plan, the entire product life cycle should be documented stating the software specifications for each stage of the product software design and development process. This should include the strategy for test, verification and validation and a report recording the same at each stage of completion.

IEC Software Criteria

Remember: Compliance is checked by inspection of the risk management file.

Since IEC 604-1-4 covers software requirements for medical electrical equipment, it is more demanding in the nature of its requirements. Other manufacturers of comparable high-risk products should consider some of the software requirements from the IEC, ISO, EU and/or appropriate trade groups when developing their software design requirements.

The following is an example from the IEC software standard:

A risk management summary must be developed throughout the life cycle of a programmable electronic medical system (PES) as a part of a Risk Management File. When complete, it shall contain:

● Identified hazards

● The cause(s) of each hazard

● Assignment of *severity*

- Estimation likelihood

- Estimation of risk

- Safety integrity levels

- Reference to the *safety measures* used to eliminate or control the risk of the *hazard*

- Reference to *verification*

- Reference to *validation.*

Risk Management Plan

Remember: Compliance is checked by inspection of the risk management file, according to requirements of IEC 604-1-4.

IEC 604-1-4, states:

The manufacturer shall prepare a risk management plan. The plan shall include the following:

- Scope of the plan, defining the project or product and the life cycle phases for which the plan is applicable

- The life cycle including verification and validation

- Management responsibilities in accordance with 4.1 of ISO 9001

- Risk/benefit criteria

- Methods for risk management

- Reviews

- If the plan changes during the course of development, a record of the changes shall be kept.

The standard goes on to detail what is meant by the life cycle, risk management process (including hazard identification), PES requirement specification, PES architecture, PES design and implementation, *verification, validation, modification and assessment.*

The conclusion of each section contains the statement:

Remember: Compliance is checked by inspection of the risk management file.

In addition to providing a tough standard for a high-risk product, this standard also provides a powerful set of questions to be directed to the manufacturer of any high-risk product containing programmable software. Naturally, comparable standards can be utilized in other product areas, where available. The key for an ISO 9000 quality management program is to document the concern for product safety in the elements that satisfy Clause 4.4, Design Control, of an ISO 9001-based QMS.

Warnings and Instructions

As the third leg of the principles of safety integration—to warn against dangers when designing out and/or guarding against dangers are not options—warnings and instructions are critical to product safety and should be an integral part of the Design Control section of any ISO 9001-based QMS.

In various US court decisions, products have been found defective and manufacturers have been held liable for the following reasons:

- If warnings are insufficient or absent.

- If instructions are needed for a consumer to understand a product beyond its apparent characteristics (i.e., additional knowledge, perhaps warning of adverse consequences, would be needed to fully understand how to use the product safely).

- If the manufacturer and/or distributor do not provide sufficient warnings about known risks, thereby encouraging or causing misuse or misleading consumers who might have acted differently if they had known about the actual risks.

- If the manufacturer and/or distributor fail to warn against known or anticipated improper uses, thereby encouraging such misuse.

- If the manufacturer and/or distributor fail to warn of foreseeable dangers in a manner understandable to the ordinary consumer or user, including the display of appropriate pictograms and/or pictographs or making this information available in the user's language.

- When a manufacturer and/or distributor fail to update warnings and instructions when necessary.

- When a manufacturer and/or distributor misbrand a product by providing false or misleading information.

- When product labels contain inadequate directions for use, thereby prompting misuse.

- When product labels do not contain accurate information concerning a product's contents, thereby prompting product misuse.

- When required product information is not prominently displayed or clearly stated, thereby causing product misuse.

- When product advertising doesn't contain appropriate information about intended uses, side effects, precautions or warnings.

The preceding list is not exhaustive, but it does provide some understanding of what can happen if warnings and instructions are misleading and/or inadequate.

Suggested Strategies

The issue of product design and product safety should be a key element in satisfying the requirements of Clause 4.4, Design Control, within an ISO 9001-based QMS. Because these issues are critical to product safety and design control, the following strategies should be considered:

- Establish a product safety committee to deal with warnings, instructions and labeling.

- Develop standard operating procedures for warnings, instructions and labeling.

- Consider intended product users or operators when developing warnings and instructions.

- Warn against known risks, including those that are obvious. Critical information should be affixed (e.g., etched, stamped or painted) so that it can't be erased or obscured after heavy use of the product.

- Clearly state contraindications and warn against improper uses.

- Provide product users with clear and concise directions, information and precautions for use.

- Show capacity ratings, safety limits, special instructions and all essential information on products in the user's language. The language should be clear and unambiguous.

- Warn about the need to maintain and repair products and provide suggested maintenance time schedules.

- Warn against improper or unapproved alteration of products and warn against any risks posed by product alterations.

- Consider periodic audits and updates of the instructions, warnings and labeling program.

- Decide if it would be appropriate to warn against product obsolescence.

- Attach working labels for products written at the education level of the user. This is especially critical for nonprofessional users of products such as machinery. Use pictograms or pictographs to aid understanding.

- On the packages containing products, do not show product usage inconsistent with the product, thereby misleading potential users.

- Print and/or affix adequate and appropriate warning labels to the package containing the product. Warnings should be affixed to the product, contained in the instructions and affixed to the packaging in the language of the consumer.

- Anticipate possible product misuse when writing and designing warnings. Include the type and seriousness of the danger(s) in the warnings and how they can be avoided. Warnings must describe what will happen if people are exposed to the danger(s). Warnings must be written in clear, concise and understandable language and include pictograms or pictographs that will communicate to illiterate users. It is important to use internationally accepted colors to make warnings visible from a safe distance. Affix critical warnings to last the lifetime of the product.

- Make sure operating instructions and maintenance manuals are clear, adequate, unambiguous and understandable to the user. Write these manuals in the user's language, so that they are readable at the educational level of the user and in a format (e.g., pictograms and drawings) that communicates the danger(s) effectively to the user.

● Develop product marketing and advertising consistent with the intended use of the product and do not mislead and/or exaggerate products to potential users.

● Create product data sheets to track instructions, warnings and labeling for each product.

● Instructional formats are critical to understanding instructions (i.e., language, photographs, international symbols, drawings, etc.).

● Include explicit warnings in marketing materials and instructions for use.

● Review all advertising with product liability and product safety in mind.

Postsale Obligations

Postsale obligations is a growing area for litigation. The requirement of the new EU Machinery Directive—"to eliminate any risk of accident throughout the foreseeable life of the machinery"— means that a manufacturer must calculate foreseeable use and misuse when designing a machine and then must monitor after-sale behavior to see if the original calculations were accurate.

The Directive further states, "When designing and constructing machinery, the manufacturer must envisage not only the normal use of the machinery, but also uses which reasonably could be expected." This means that the calculation of foreseeable use and misuse is continuous and evolving.

In effect, product designers and/or their support personnel (i.e., product safety committee, safety review panel, etc.) need to consider postsale obligations and postsale activities when designing new products. (ISO 9004-1 discusses the issue of product traceability.)

If a company wishes to provide product warranties and/or guarantees, competent legal advisors should closely review any contractual obligations for direct and implied legal commitments. Misleading or meaningless language that commits a company to little or nothing may not sit well with a court. Such attempts to lure customers with empty promises may result in punitive damages in a liability lawsuit. It would be wiser to offer a meaningful warranty/ guarantee or offer nothing, rather than offer something misleading.

A defense attorney who specializes in medical device product liability lawsuits commented, "A complaint is any statement of dissatisfaction about a product from anyone!" He goes on to say that all complaints, however annoying, must be given serious attention.

Whichever person(s) handles the customer feedback systems must be trained to receive and record the information objectively, in a neutral fashion, and not project the problem back on the customer/user. In addition to making an effort to keep customer dissatisfaction at a minimum level, it is legally unwise to turn customer service over to inept personnel whose behavior might provoke a lawsuit.

Complaints

As noted in ISO 9004-1, customer complaints provide both a good service and create a valuable feedback loop for product use, misuse, potential modifications and redesigns. This all helps to create a better product and reduce liability exposure.

To take advantage of complaints, as recommended by ISO 9004-1, companies should:

- Develop procedures to record and categorize complaints and compile them in a central record for review.

- Develop procedures and systematize responses to investigate, analyze and respond to complaints.

- Carefully train customer service personnel to record and respond to complaints.

- Carefully train service and repair personnel and/or contract service personnel to record and respond to complaints.

- Develop internal procedures to review and categorize complaints and forward the information to appropriate company personnel (e.g., research, design, legal, management, manufacturing/ production, quality control and product safety committee).

- Identify responsibilities for complaint reviews and response committee (e.g., redesigns and reengineering), manufacturing/ production, product safety committee, management, quality control, legal, etc.

● Develop and follow carefully documented procedures for implementing changes.

Recalls

Recalls also provide a product service and feedback loop for product modifications and redesigns, as noted in ISO 9004-1. More importantly, recalls provide a critical element in a product liability control program to demonstrate responsible behavior and a commitment to product safety. A product recall system should:

● Provide for ongoing product performance evaluation and complaint evaluation.

● Review and update product information on a regular basis.

● Maintain appropriate records to facilitate a product recall should one become necessary.

● Devise a contingency plan and set aside financial resources should this step be necessary.

● Develop a plan to deal with the public and press should a product recall become necessary.

● Review, update and continuously revise the contingency plan.

Postsale obligations are anticipated in several industries and often are mandated in regulated industries in the US and EU. Whatever the reasons, companies should be prepared to act swiftly on a product recall for purposes of product safety and customer satisfaction.

In addition, a company should rehearse its emergency preparedness plan. When a recall occurs, the pressure from the public and the media can create a crisis setting in which panic rules. It would be wise to build complaints and recalls into an ISO 9001-based QMS, incorporating ideas from ISO 9004-1 and a postsale obligation program.

Component Parts

Approximately 35 percent of all product liability lawsuits involve component parts. Whether a company designs and contracts for components with subcontractors, purchases component parts "off the shelf", is itself a supplier to an end manufacturer as a subcontractor or sells component parts in the marketplace, how this issue is dealt with in an ISO 9001-based QMS will affect a company's degree of liability exposure.

Already, companies such as Dow and DuPont have announced that they no longer will supply basic materials to medical device manufacturers. These suppliers of basic component materials have grown tired of serving as "deep pockets" in device liability lawsuits.

ISO 9001 & Component Parts

ISO 9001 deals with component parts in Subclause 4.6.2, Evaluation of Subcontractors, which is amplified by ISO 9004-1, Clauses 9.1, Quality in Purchasing, 9.5, Agreement on Verification Methods, and 9.6, Provisions for Settlement of Disputes. The area of purchasing is dealt with in ISO 9001 by Subclause 4.6.3, Purchasing Data, and in ISO 9004-1 by Clauses 9.2, Requirements for Specifications, Drawings and Purchase Documents, and 9.4, Agreement on Quality Assurance.

Buyer & Seller Liability Exposure

The issue of liability exposure exists at two different levels on either side of the buyer/seller equation. Companies that design products and subcontract their raw materials and component parts need to clearly specify their quality requirements. Ideally, at a minimum subcontractors should have an ISO 9001/2/3-based quality system in place to assure consistency in quality between part 1 and part 21,469.

If a manufacturer is buying component parts for a machine to be CE-marked for sale in the EU, a quality system would be a requirement for "series manufacture" and the component parts company also would have to guarantee that European safety standards have been met by providing either an **EC Declaration of Conformity** or an **EC Declaration of Incorporation**, depending on the nature of the component part. *Note: "series manufacture" refers to production of everything but one-of-a-kind machines.*

The Declaration of Conformity is the piece of paper that must accompany *all* CE-marked products into the EU. A Declaration of

Incorporation must accompany those products that cannot be CE-marked but must be compliant with the requirements of the Machinery Directive.

If a manufacturer is buying component parts "off the shelf", it will need to make certain that it has sufficient information to safely add the component part to its end product. Again, if the "off-the-shelf" component part were headed to the EU, it would have to be CE-marked (if that were legally required) and be accompanied by either an EC Declaration of Conformity or not CE-marked, but accompanied by a Declaration of Incorporation, depending on the nature of the component part. In addition, it would help an "off-the-shelf" buyer if the component part came from a company with a registered ISO 9001/2/3-based quality system.

If a company manufactures component parts to end-user design requirements, it is critical that design specifications be adequately detailed. In legal jurisdictions such as the EU, this would allow a component parts manufacturer to use the EU Product Liability Directive, Article 7, to escape liability "if [the manufacturer] proves (f) in the case of a manufacturer of a component, that the defect is attributable to the design of the product in which the component has been fitted or to the instructions given by the manufacturer of the product." Whether this exemption would be available to a US defendant would depend on the vagaries of US product liability law on a state-by-state basis. (If a component part supplier suspected or had evidence that the end use compromised the integrity of the component part and did nothing to raise the issue, most likely the company would be liable in both EU and US jurisdictions.)

If a company manufactures component parts for general sale in the marketplace that will be purchased off the shelf by multiple end users, it is critical that all tolerances and operating limits be identified clearly. Otherwise, the component parts manufacturer will have failed to warn of limitations and could be liable for not providing adequate warnings and instructions:

Component Part Considerations

The following points should be considered when building a component parts monitoring system:

- It is critical that purchased materials, supplies and components be logged in at the time and date of receipt to establish the separate and distinct nature of "bought-in components". Failure to accomplish this logging procedure will "marry" components with end products, "marry" the liability of contractors and subcontractors and eliminate the legal opportunity to establish a separate identity and liability for separate contributions. *Note: "Subcontractor" refers to any entity providing materials or services to the supplier.* Conversely, it will make it difficult—if not impossible—for end manufacturers to determine whether subcontractors had complied with contractor specifications.

- For purposes of liability control, it is critical to make sure that:

  ○ Subcontractors are identified.

  ○ Subcontractor-written specifications are provided at a level of detail sufficient to guarantee acceptable quality.

  ○ Subcontractor supplies are tested for acceptable quality (either by the contractor or via a third-party quality assessment).

  ○ Subcontractor materials and bought-in components are identified to determine if they are acceptable.

  ○ Subcontractors understand the use of materials and bought-in components.

- Care should be taken to clearly identify products to limit the liability exposure of both the manufacturer and component parts subcontractor.

- Manufacturers should maintain records of any "customer-supplied products" to create a paper trail that clearly separates the customer from the manufacturer.

- Manufacturers should create and maintain procedures that identify the product during all stages of production, delivery and installation to assure liability control and maintain traceability.

- Special care should be given to continuous monitoring and compliance with documented procedures to assure that specified requirements provide adequate product liability documentation.

- Each of these points represents key aspects of ISO 9001, among them Clause 4.6, Purchasing.

Summary

Going Beyond ISO 9004-1

While it is critical that every clause of ISO 9004-1 be addressed and, where relevant, folded into an ISO 9001-based QMS, this alone does not create a preventive law program addressing all of the key issues relevant to liability exposure.

Preventive law is an emerging discipline that addresses key issues in records management and documentation, product design (including risk assessment and risk management), product design and software (where relevant), warnings and instructions, postsale obligations (often called postsale surveillance, postsale monitoring or postsale tracking) and component parts.

There are many issues and questions that need to be addressed in examining an ISO 9001/2-based QMS, examples of which are presented in this chapter. Each issue can be expanded and must be tailored to the product and/or service in question.

The Importance of a Preventive Law Program

Note: This company now has a preventive law program, is registered to ISO 9001 and has CE-marked its product under three new approach safety directives (Machinery, Electromagnetic Compatibility and Low Voltage) for sale in the EU.

As noted in the section on design and software, a machinery manufacturer of "one-of-a-kind machines" discovered that a customer's employee caught his arm in an auger, resulting in serious injury.

The employee (plaintiff) sued his employer and the machine manufacturer, and the plaintiff's attorney discovered that the manufacturer could not accurately identify the operating software for the machine. Apparently, since each machine was "one-of-a-kind," the engineers created "one-of-a-kind" software without ever identifying the variable characteristics of each software package or keeping a backup copy of the software in the plant. Consequently, the argument that "the software did it" could not be refuted, and the case was settled out of court for six figures in damages awarded to the plaintiff.

A specific, documented product design procedure for software, built into an ISO 9001-based QMS, would have provided document control and would have answered whether the software failed to provide adequate safety or the incident was caused by operator error. While it might or might not have prevented the manufacturer from incurring a liability loss, it could have reduced the amount of the claim/award.

Chapter V

ISO 9000 & the Harmonization of National Laws

OVERVIEW

The ISO 9000 series is playing a major role in the harmonization of national laws as trade barriers disappear and international trade increases. It is an essential part of the globalization of laws and standards as an increasing number of governments accept it as a useful tool.

This chapter will focus on the relationship of ISO 9000 to countries and industries around the world.

KEY POINTS

Important: The use of ISO 9000 in medical device regulation is far more complex than a conventional ISO 9000 QMS. To understand, defend or attack such a program, it is necessary for attorneys to understand its application in the regulatory process and the future role of ISO 13485 and ISO 13488.

Important: Attorneys will need to become familiar with ISO 14001 because it will be used in conjunction with ISO 9000 and, more important, it likely will be used by companies to help satisfy certain EPA policies.

❖ To provide effective legal counsel, attorneys will need to understand the basic structure of ISO 9000 and its product- and/or service-specific applications to a client.

❖ The ISO 9000 series of standards is an integral part of the EU's modular approach as applied in its "new approach" safety directives.

❖ The EU's "new approach" delineates the essential safety requirements in each directive and sets forth conformity assessment procedures.

❖ ISO 9001/2/3 registration *is not* a requirement for exporting to the EU.

❖ Some European countries are stipulating ISO 9001/2/3 registration as a requirement to bid on government procurement contracts.

❖ The CE mark is a European seal of approval, designating that the product meets certain health and safety requirements.

❖ ISO 9001/2/3 *is not* the sole requirement for CE-marking products and machinery in the EU.

❖ As with ISO 9000, CE-marking alone will not provide adequate legal defense in the face of a liability lawsuit.

❖ CE-marked products contain specific and detailed information about product safety compliance, meaning that CE-marking information is available through legal discovery.

❖ ISO 14000 is a series of environmental management system standards that may affect companies satisfying environmental regulations.

❖ QS-9000 is ISO 9001 tailored to the needs of the automotive industry.

ISO 9000 & European Law

The Standards and Harmonization

As a group, the Member States of the European Union (EU) have the largest number and percentage of global ISO 9001/2/3 registrations (the Europeans use the term "certifications"). While the largest percentage of these registrations has been driven by the private marketplace, the best-known, most discussed and least understood application of ISO 9001/2/3 registration has come from its use as a conformity assessment procedure option to demonstrate compliance with the safety requirements in those industries affected by the EU's new approach directives.

Misconceptions About ISO 9000 & the EU

Beginning in 1990, several US consultants made extravagant statements that ISO 9001/2/3 registration was a requirement for exporting products to the EU (not true). To this was added the statement that ISO 9001/2/3 registration was the only requirement for CE-marking of products such as medical devices and machinery for the EU (also, not true). (CE is *Conformité Européenne* in French, or *European Conformity* in English.)

What caused this mix of misinformation and entrepreneurial zeal by people wanting to market their professional expertise isn't clear, but vestiges of this mix of fiction and fact linger today. Unfortunately, it has caused several companies to make misinformed business decisions—e.g., US medical device companies that registered to ISO 9001/2/3 and then called to ask where they could "buy their CE marks".

The EU White Paper—Beginnings of Harmonization

First Step in Eliminating Barriers

In March 1985, the European Commission submitted *Completing the Internal Market: White Paper from the Commission of the European Council*, which the Council approved and published in June 1985. It contained 300 pieces of legislation (later reduced to 286) that pledged to eliminate fiscal, technical and physical barriers within the EU by:

- Replacing national standards with European Community-wide standards

- Eliminating Member-State regulations that restrict trade (i.e., health, safety and environmental regulations)

- Agreeing on EC-wide testing and certification procedures.

The purpose of the White Paper grew out of a need to open up the country-to-country market among the 12 EU Member States (then called the European Community). Even though market trade among EU States had increased since the European Court of Justice (ECJ) announced its *Casis dé Dijon* decision on *mutual recognition* in 1979, the court acknowledged that Member States could restrict the entry of any products that presented health, safety or environmental threats. Since these constraints affected 60 percent of all products traded among EU Member States, the White Paper was needed to create EU-wide legislation dealing with health, safety and environmental requirements that would become a part of each country's national law, thereby eliminating national trade barriers.

The New Approach Directives

Among the 286 directives adopted were laws affecting toy safety, machinery safety, electromagnetic compatibility, low voltage medical devices, etc. Instead of following the "old approach" to safety legislation covering products—e.g., chemicals and pharmaceuticals—where everything needed for compliance was spelled out in the directive, a "new approach" was introduced.

The "new approach" directive created a basic framework that delineated the *essential safety requirements*, set forth the *conformity assessment procedures* and turned over the writing of EN-harmonized (European Norm) safety standards to two European regional standards organizations—CEN (European Committee for Standardization) and CENELEC (European Committee for Electrotechnical Standardization). These quasi-governmental organizations are comprised of representatives from national standards authorities (e.g., AFNOR-French, BSI-British, DIN-German), manufacturing, universities and consumer groups from 18 of the 19 EU and EFTA (European Free Trade Association) nations. (The only country not represented is Liechtenstein.) Two of these EU new approach directives are reprinted in Appendices B and C.

Technical Harmonization Efforts

The magnitude of the EN-harmonized safety standards effort is huge. For example, to develop the essential safety standards for CE-marking to the EU Machinery Directive, 40 CEN committees have written or are in the process of writing 650 safety standards. More than 400 safety standards are being developed for the Personal Protective Equipment Directive, which deals with protective clothing used in dangerous environments.

Safety Directive Compliance & CE-Marking

To comply with an EU new approach safety directive, it is necessary to study the mandatory essential safety requirements to determine which apply to your company's or client's product(s), identify which of the EN-harmonized safety standards (or alternative safety standards) demonstrate that your product(s) satisfies the essential requirements and then select a conformity assessment procedure specified in a directive to record your compliance.

Depending upon your product and the directive(s) that applies to it, this may involve testing and/or quality assurance approval by an EU-notified body (a European third party that must be approved by a national accrediting body within the EU to certify products for a specific directive).

Once this is accomplished, a company must affix a CE mark and issue a Declaration of Conformity in order for the product to be sold legally in the European Union.

ISO 9000 & the New Approach Directives

It is at the level of conformity assessment procedures that ISO 9000 comes into play with the EU new approach safety directives. As the first directives were being drafted, the European Commission articulated its initial ideas with a formal European Council Resolution—*Global Approach to Certification and Testing*—on December 21, 1989, in response to the 1985 White Paper. This was followed a year later on December 13, 1990, with a Council Decision (90/683/EEC) entitled *Concerning the Modules for the Various Phases of Conformity Assessment Which Are Intended to Be Used in the Technical Harmonization Directives*. Three years later this decision was revised to develop uniform rules for CE-marking in a Council Decision (93/465/EEC) of July 22, 1993, entitled *Concerning the Modules for the Various Phases of Conformity Assessment Procedures and the Rules for the Affixing and Use of the CE Conformity Marking Which Are Intended to Be Used in the Technical Harmonization Directives.*

Approved and Proposed New Approach Directives

For those who don't understand the origins, purpose or application of CE-marking to various products, the most confusing aspect is the breadth of products that must be CE-marked *and* the different product safety and process quality criteria necessary to accomplish this objective, since the requirements vary widely by directive. The following is a list of just a few of the 286 approved and proposed EU directives, of which one or more may apply to a product:

- Toy Safety Directive 88/378/EEC as Amended by 93/68/EEC

- Directive on Construction Products 89/106/EEC as Amended by 93/68/EEC and Augmented by Council Decision 94/611/EC & 96/603/EC

- Directive on Telecommunications Terminal Equipment 91/263/EEC as Amended by 93/68/EEC

- Electromagnetic Compatibility Directive 89/336/EEC as Amended by 92/31/EEC & 93/68/EEC

- Machinery Directive 89/392/EEC as Amended by 91/368/EEC, 93/44/EEC & 93/68/EEC

- Low Voltage Directive 72/23/EEC as Amended by 93/68/EEC

- Active Implantable Medical Devices Directive 90/385/EEC as Amended by 93/42/EEC & 93/68/EEC

- Medical Devices Directive 93/42/EEC

- Directive on Personal Protective Equipment 89/686/EEC as Amended by 93/68/EEC, 93/95/EEC & 96/58/EC

- Directive on Efficiency Requirements for New Hot-Water Boilers Fired With Liquid and Gaseous Fuels 92/42/EEC as Amended by 93/68/EEC

- Directive on Appliances Burning Gaseous Fuels 90/396/EEC as Amended by 93/68/EEC

- Directive on Simple Pressure Vessels 87/404/EEC as Amended by 90/488/EEC and 93/68/EEC

- Directive Concerning Equipment and Protective Systems Intended for Use in Potentially Explosive Atmospheres 94/9/EC

- Directive on Satellite Earth Station Equipment 93/97/EEC Supplementing the EU Directive on Telecommunications Terminal Equipment (TTE) 91/263/EEC as Amended by 93/68/EEC

- Directive on Recreational Craft 94/24/EC

- Directive on Non-Automatic Weighing Instruments 90/384/EEC as Amended by 93/68/EEC

- Directive Relating to Lifts 95/16/EC

- Proposed In Vitro Diagnostic Medical Devices Directive 95/C 172/02

- Proposed Directive on Marine Equipment 95/C 218/06

- Proposed Directive Relating to Cableway Installations Designed to Carry Passengers 94/C 70/07

- Directive Concerning Pressure Equipment 97/23/EC

- Commission Directive 95/54/EC Adapting to Technical Progress, Council Directive 72/245 Relating to the Suppression of Radio Emission Interference Produced by Spark Ignition Engines Fitted to Motor Vehicles and Amending Directive 70/156/EEC Relating to the Type Approval of Motor Vehicles and Their Trailers as Clarified by Commission Communication (96/C 285/06) Relating to the Electromagnetic Compatibility of Vehicles and Associated Components.

Modular Approach to Conformity Assessment

In the modular approach, the EU identified eight possible modules for complying with a directive. Therefore, when a new directive is in the working draft stage, the drafters select which of the eight modules will be used as conformity assessment procedures for a specific directive. The modules range all the way from a formal manufacturer self-declaration of conformity to a full quality assurance system approved by an EU-notified body. The choice of modules depends on the degree of safety risk presented by the product. A few points for attorneys and the companies they represent to remember are:

- Of the eight modules contained in the modular approach, one is full quality assurance (i.e., ISO 9001) and stands alone and two—"production quality assurance" (i.e., ISO 9002) and "product quality assurance" (i.e., ISO 9003)—must be used in conjunction with the EC-Type Examination module, which covers product design and requires that an EC-Type Examination Certificate be received from a notified body before complying with either ISO 9002 or ISO 9003.

- The EU always includes non-ISO 9000 choices for complying with new approach product safety directives.

- Whenever a company certifies to an ISO 9000 conformity assessment procedure for an EU new approach safety directive, it always involves complying with essential safety requirements and product safety standards as a part of the conformity assessment process (i.e., product safety is always a part of the quality assurance system, which also may involve a technical file and notified body approval).

- For some directives, such as the three EU medical devices directives (Active Implantable Medical Devices Directive, Medical Devices Directive and the proposed In Vitro Diagnostic Medical Devices Directive), the EU augmented the generic structure of ISO 9001 and ISO 9002 with EN46001 and EN46002, which are designed to apply ISO 9001 and ISO 9002, respectively, to medical devices. In addition, the EU created guidance documents, EN50103 for Active Implantable Medical Devices, EN724 for Medical Devices and EN928 for In Vitro Diagnostic Medical Devices to guide the combining of ISO 9000 with EN46000 for each of the three types of medical devices. Finally, each of these EN guidance documents references specific clauses from ISO 9004-1 on a clause-by-clause basis. (This development of augmenting the basic ISO 9000 structure to apply to specific products is quite significant and will be discussed again later in this chapter.)

- Since the EU allows each company to choose its preferred conformity assessment procedure and method of conformity, conformity assessment is considered voluntary and a "government made me do it" US-style preemption defense is not available in the EU legal structure.

- Some of the early directives such as the EU Toy Safety and Electromagnetic Compatibility Directives were adopted prior to the development of the modular approach and do not have ISO 9000 conformity assessment procedures as a method for complying with the directives.

- The EU Machinery Directive also precedes the development of the modular approach and does not offer an ISO 9000 conformity assessment procedure. However, it does require that a technical file be created. This file must contain a listing of all the essential requirements that apply to the product in question (including product tests, drawings and operating instructions) as well as a quality manual. For series manufacture, it also must identify the quality system that assures quality in manufacturing. *Note: "series manufacture" refers to production of everything but one-of-a-kind machines.* While it need not be ISO 9001/2/ 3, it must be a real quality system.

- All new approach directives, beginning in late 1989 and early 1990 (e.g., Active Implantable Medical Devices Directive) utilized the modular approach in developing their conformity assessment procedures.

- CE-marked products that use ISO 9001/2/3 as a method of conformity assessment also must satisfy other product-specific safety requirements and compliance requirements that must be examined to fully understand the nature of the quality system. For defense attorneys, it means that CE-marked products contain specific and detailed information about product safety compliance. For plaintiff's attorneys, it means that CE-marking information is available through legal discovery and that compliance must be examined alongside product standards to see if the company actually complied with those standards. This is especially true where manufacturers self-certify to directives such as Machinery and Toy Safety. [Legal discovery produces data and/or documents that one party to a legal action is compelled to disclose to another party either prior to or during a legal proceeding.]

- Not all CE-marking is the same, even with high-risk products such as medical devices. Recently, the FDA forced a US medical device manufacturer to sign a consent decree or face civil and criminal action and closure of the manufacturing facility. Since the device also was CE-marked and had not been pulled from circulation in the EU, it raised serious questions about the quality management function and the medical expertise function of the EU-notified body. Clearly, the issue raised liability concerns for both the manufacturer and the notified body that approved the CE mark.

ISO 9000 & EU Government Procurement Contracts

Just as the Europeans have been adopting ISO 9001/2/3 in the marketplace and have been using ISO 9001/2/3 as part of the modular approach in their new approach safety directives, EU governments have been requiring ISO 9001/2/3 registration for government bids and procurement contracts. This means that when Ford Motor Company wants to compete for contracts for the motor pool of a UK government agency, it must be ISO 9001/2/3-registered to submit a bid. Whether it is a food contract to the French government, a machinery contract to the Danish government or a clothing contract to the German military, a competing company must be ISO 9001/2/3-registered. In addition, countries that expect to join the EU in the future also are requiring ISO 9001/2/3 registration for government procurement contracts. In 1995, the Polish government began stipulating ISO 9001/2/3 registration as a requirement for procurement contracts.

ISO 9000 and International Law

IMO & ISO 9000—Harmonization Efforts

International Maritime Organization (IMO) and International Management Code for the Safe Operation of Ships and for Pollution Prevention (ISM Code)

In a related move initiated in 1994, the ISM Code has adopted a version of ISO 9002 with the objective of "ensuring safety at sea, prevention of human injury or loss of life, and avoidance of damage to the environment, in particular, to the marine environment and to property" (ISM Code 1.2.1). This version of ISO 9002 is identified as *Marine Management and Ship Operation Guideline ISO 9002/ISM Code.*

As with other versions of ISO 9001/2/3 for regulated industries, the standard has been tailored to meet the unique needs of the maritime industry, in particular the operation of ships at sea. Further, it isn't a voluntary standard, it is a mandatory standard of the IMO. Since pollution prevention also is a concern, this standard includes environmental management and pollution prevention as a part of the ISO 9002/ISM Code.

ISO 9000 and US Law

ISO 9000 & US Government Procurement Contracts

As noted in Chapter I, ISO 9000 can trace its origins directly back to the US Military and efforts by the Department of Defense (DoD) to exercise quality control over the procurement of supplies and equipment from defense contractors. That such controls are necessary can be reaffirmed by reading the *Wall Street Journal,* February 27, 1996, which listed the most recent egregious efforts by a few defense contractors to falsify quality records and defraud the government.

Several noteworthy recent violations to quality control regulations include:

- Supplying defective bolts, which failed to adequately secure Maverick Missiles to aircraft wings

- Supplying defective gearboxes for electrical, oil and fuel systems on Navy F-18 fighters

- Failing to properly service emergency equipment on Air Force One and Two

- Submitting false tests for resistors, which failed to properly control electrical current in weapons systems.

Since these cases of fraud against the US Military compromised national security and could have cost human lives, there is reason to hope that the combination of court imposed financial penalties and prison terms will create sufficient disincentives to circumvent quality control procedures in the future.

The move by the DoD to accept ISO 9000 quality management system standards in lieu of military quality assurance standards brings the process full circle. While there was some initial hesitation to abandon "MIL-Q" standards, the increasing use of ISO 9000 in the marketplace by defense-related industries as well as its adoption by NATO and defense departments of NATO Member States made the decision to adopt a common quality system too compelling to resist.

Further, since procurement contracts can shape the application of ISO 9000 through standards contract requirements, DoD didn't forfeit any of its quality control concerns.

In 1995, both DoD and NASA announced their intentions to develop procurement requirements using common quality system requirements based on ISO 9000. The mechanism for accomplishing this objective was a Memorandum of Understanding (MOU) focusing on a common quality process among government agencies. In addition to DoD and NASA, 10 other government agencies signed the MOU, including the Army, Navy, Air Force, Defense Contract Management Command, Coast Guard, National Institute of Standards and Technology, National Oceanic and Atmospheric Administration, Maritime Administration, General Services Administration and Federal Aviation Administration. It is reasonable to expect that the number of US government agencies adopting ISO 9001/2/3 registration as a procurement requirement will increase in the future.

The FDA, QSR & ISO 9000

US Food and Drug Administration (FDA) Harmonization of Its *Quality System Regulation* (QSR) with EU Medical Device Directives and ISO 9000

One application of ISO 9000 to regulated industries that is especially interesting is the FDA's harmonization of its QSR—issued September 1996, which took effect June 1997—with the EU's use of ISO 9001/2/3 to regulate medical devices. It is interesting on three counts. First, a considerable part of the EU approach to medical device regulation is derived from the FDA's previous Good Manufacturing Practices (GMPs). While the EU broke the FDA's regulatory structure into three medical device regulations and developed a public/private procedure to approach medical device regulation (i.e., government accreditation and regulation of private third-party notified bodies), it is an FDA-style structure.

Second, the ISO 9001/2/3 application to medical device regulation has been attractive to the FDA because it incorporates a stronger commitment to design control than existed in the FDA GMPs. Third, the FDA has been active in harmonizing its efforts with the EU and other participants in global medical device regulation, notably Australia, Canada and Japan.

Because the ISO 9000 series of standards is internationally copyrighted and therefore cannot be reprinted in the *Federal Register* and because the FDA has replaced the GMP structure with the QSR, the FDA incorporation of ISO 9001 does not follow the ISO 9001 numbered clauses; instead the FDA QSR will be found in 21 CFR §820. (Cross-references between ISO 9001 and EN46001 and 21 CFR §820 can be obtained from the FDA.) The so-called "new GMPs", *Quality System Regulation*, was published in the *Federal Register* on October 7, 1996, pages 1-67.

US and EU Sign Mutual Recognition Agreement

In June 1997, the US and EU signed a formal Mutual Recognition Agreement (MRA) covering six product sectors: electrical safety; electromagnetic compatibility (EMC); medical devices; pharmaceutical good manufacturing practices (GMPs); recreational craft; and telecommunications.

For medical devices, the US and EU have agreed to designate Conformity Assessment Bodies (CABs) to conduct the following types of reports that will be considered equivalent by both the US and EU:

a. Under the US system, surveillance/postmarket and initial/preapproval reports

b. Under the US system, premarket (510K) product evaluation reports

c. Under the EC system (in this document, the EU is identified as the European Community), quality system evaluation reports

d. Under the EC system, EC-type examination and verification reports.

The CAB assessments by US- and EU-designated CABs will be considered to be equivalent. According to the MRA, this means that:

> CABs in the EC are capable of conducting product and quality systems evaluations against US regulatory requirements in a manner equivalent to those conducted by the FDA; and CABs in the US are capable of conducting product and quality systems evaluations against EC regulatory requirements in a manner equivalent to those conducted by EC CABs.

Note that while the US will have to designate CABs, EU CABs would be the existing EU-notified bodies that have been designated for the appropriate medical devices directives by EU Member State competent authorities.

There are three components to the MRA, each covering a discrete range of products:

1. Quality System Evaluations—US-type surveillance/postmarket and initial/pre-approval inspection reports and EC-type quality system evaluation reports will be exchanged with regard to all products regulated under both US and EU law as medical devices.

2. Product Evaluation—US-type premarket (510(K)) product evaluation reports and EC-type-testing reports will be exchanged only with regard to those products classified under the US system as Class I/Class II-Tier 2 Medical Devices that are listed in Appendix 2.

3. Postmarket Vigilance Reports—Postmarket vigilance reports will be exchanged with regard to all products regulated under both US and EC law as medical devices.

Additional products and procedures may be made subject to this MRA medical devices annex of both the US and EU.

FDA Use of Third-Party Registration

In addition to working with the Europeans and the global medical device regulation community, the FDA is interested is using third-party registration on a limited experimental basis. Most likely, the first efforts would begin with lower risk devices. The obvious lure would be the ability to privatize part of the regulatory process, yet still keep it under direct FDA supervision. The problem will be controlling the quality of third-party registrars to make certain that the CE-marking breakdown between medical device regulation and quality system certification that occurred in the UK doesn't occur in the US.

Important: The use of ISO 9001 in medical device regulation is far more complex than a conventional ISO 9001/2/3-based QMS. To understand, defend or attack such a program, it is necessary for attorneys to understand its application in the regulatory process.

ISO 9000 & Global Medical Device Regulation

The FDA, in concert with Australia, Canada, the EU and Japan, has been actively involved in global medical device regulation. To this end, the FDA has been actively participating in the translation of the European medical device structure to a global ISO medical device structure.

Part of the motivation to attain this objective grew out of a close working relationship between medical device manufacturers, government regulatory bodies (such as the FDA) and US/EU medical device trade associations, and part of the motivation came from the international momentum that grew out of the EU's new medical device initiatives.

International Push to Standardize

In particular, after being chastised by the international community for developing new toy safety standards without consulting existing ISO toy safety standards, CEN signed the Vienna Agreement in 1991, promising to work in concert with ISO and create safety standards common to both the EU and ISO wherever feasible. The conclusion of this joint standards effort would be a parallel CEN/ISO vote on a common standard. At the conclusion of a CEN/ISO joint ballot, a new safety standard would become both a CEN and ISO standard.

The first such parallel vote occurred in 1993 as a result of CEN's preliminary standards EN46001 and EN46002 (the application of ISO 9001 and ISO 9002 to medical devices). The committee selected to vote on behalf of ISO was Technical Committee (TC) 176, the TC that created the ISO 9000 quality management system standards series (see the introduction to Chapter I). While this met the spirit and intent of the Vienna Agreement, TC 176 had no subject matter expertise with medical devices.

In response to this concern, ISO created a new committee, TC 210—General Aspects for Health Care Products, which received the results of the EN46000 ballot and took it under advisement. The Secretariat for TC 210 was awarded to the American National Standards Institute (ANSI), which delegated chairmanship of the committee to the Association for the Advancement of Medical Instrumentation (AAMI).

TC 210 also received the work of another international committee, the Global Harmonization Task Force, a joint effort by regulatory representatives from Canada, the EU, Japan and the US to create a new single medical device guidance document integrating the three existing EU guidance documents: EN50103 for Active Implantable Medical Devices, EN724 for Medical Devices and EN928 for In Vitro Diagnostic Medical Devices.

With the close collaboration of manufacturers, consultants, personnel from regulatory agencies and medical device trade associations, TC 210 has created international medical device quality standards to replace national standards. The core of this effort is the application of ISO 9001 and ISO 9002 to medical devices. The EN46000 series may be replaced by ISO 13485 (EN46001) and ISO 13488 (EN46002) now that they have been finalized as International Standards and published by ISO in December 1996. The three EN guidance documents (EN50103, EN724 and EN928) have been incorporated into ISO 14969, and the EU assessment standard (EN1441) has become ISO 14971.

The importance of this effort is its potential global impact. Already, Australia has initiated a Mutual Recognition Agreement (MRA) with the EU, adopting the EU medical devices directive structure. Canada has also done so, and it appears that Brazil may do the same. Although the EU has indicated that it too will eventually direct medical device manufacturers to use ISO 13485 and ISO 13488 in place of EN46001 and EN46002 respectively as options in satisfying quality system requirements for the three EU medical devices directives, the EU has not yet indicated when it will modify these directives to recognize and use the ISO standards instead of EN46001 and EN46002. Finally, the FDA has been an active participant in this process, and US-based medical device manufacturers should plan to use the ISO guidance document 14969 and the risk assessment standard 14971 that have augmented and been referenced in the FDA guidance language for the new ISO 9001-based QSR. The FDA's commitment to global harmonization can be found in the *Federal Register* (October 11, 1995, pages 53078-53084).

For US lawyers, this means that if you intend to practice in this area, you will need to master the impact of ISO 9000 on medical device companies to better serve your clients. It also means that it is necessary to understand both the QMS and the safety requirements for the products being manufactured.

ISO 14000—Environmental Management Systems

Another ongoing situation that parallels the ISO 9000 quality management systems series is development of the ISO 14000 environmental management systems (EMS) standards series. The push to develop ISO 14000 grew out of the EU's Eco-Management and Audit Scheme (EMAS) that was adopted in July 1993, and is ISO's response to the Rio Summit in 1992. While EMAS is a voluntary EMS scheme that was designed to involve participation by industrial sites within EU Member States, there was a concern that EMAS would become mandatory and that the EU would adopt its own environmental standard and pressure the international community to accept it as a new ISO standard. Indeed, with the UK's development and release of its own EMS standard—BS 7750—in March 1992, the UK was testing BS 7750 and was putting it forth for consideration by the EU very early in the process. Further, BS 7750 had created a crosswalk matrix with ISO 9001 to make the concept more attractive.

To avoid having another international standard follow the same path as ISO 9000 (BS 5750 to ISO 9000, see Chapter I), ISO created TC 207 to deal with environmental issues and placed the Secretariat in Canada. In addition, the member bodies of ISO asked the EU to allow TC 207 to complete its work on ISO 14000 and consider adopting ISO 14000 as a key optional component in the EU's Eco-Management and Audit Scheme. This was acceptable to the EU provided that TC 207 completed its work by mid-1996. In particular, representatives from the US (e.g., manufacturers,

EPA, consultants) didn't want to experience a new international standard in which they didn't have a full voice.

The ISO 14000 series has become the new EMS set of standards. Its two basic documents are *ISO 14001, Environmental Management Systems—Specification With Guidance for Use*, a single conformance standard, and *ISO 14004, Environmental Management Systems—General Guidelines on Principles, Systems and Supporting Techniques*, the general guidance standard (similar to ISO 9004-1). They were published in September 1996 and were quickly followed by ISO 14010, ISO 14011 and ISO 14012, the Guidelines for Environmental Auditing standards, in October 1996. Although the number of sites registered to ISO 14001 is still small compared with ISO 9001/2/3, the pace is significantly higher in the US and worldwide compared with ISO 9000's introduction in 1987.

In April 1997, the European Council formally recognized that ISO 14001 is "equivalent" to EMAS, which has led to the development of a bridge annex by the CEN that specifies additional requirements for an ISO 14001-registered site to conform to EMAS's registration requirements.

Important: Attorneys will need to become familiar with ISO 14001 because it will be used in conjunction with ISO 9000. More important, ISO 14001 likely will be used by companies to satisfy the EPA Policy, *Incentives for Self-Policing: Discovery, Disclosure, Correction and Prevention of Violations*, in the *Federal Register*, December 22, 1995.

QS-9000 & the Automotive Industry

While *Quality System Requirements QS-9000* implementation and registration are being driven by the marketplace, its magnitude and the fact that the Big Three require QS-9000 "certification" of the quality systems of their production and service part suppliers (8,000 to 9,000 are required to achieve registration) make it comparable to a regulatory requirement. The Big Three define "certification" in two ways:

1. Chrysler Corporation and General Motors require production and service part suppliers to achieve third-party registration of

their quality systems to QS-9000 by set deadlines (Chrysler's was July 31, 1997, and GM's was December 31, 1997).

2. Ford Motor Company has required its North American suppliers to be in *compliance* with QS-9000 since June 1995. This involves a self-assessment, identification of all nonconformance issues and a work plan to address these issues. Ford retains the right to contact a supplier if it wishes to see the supplier's self-assessment or conduct an on-site second-party audit of the supplier's quality system.

In addition, the Big Three have created a supplemental standard, *Quality System Requirements: Tooling & Equipment Supplement* (TE Supplement), which replaced Chrysler's Tooling and Equipment Supplier Quality Assurance (TESQA) and Ford's Facilities and Tool Quality System Standard (F&T QSS). It provides guidance on the application of the requirements of QS-9000 as they relate to tooling and equipment (TE) suppliers. The TE Supplement is voluntary for the time being (a TE supplier cannot register to the TE Supplement at present), but it is expected to become a mandatory requirement within the next few years. Ford has already established deadlines of December 1998 and December 1999 for 600 "key" TE suppliers to achieve registration to ISO 9001/2 with use of the *Reliability & Maintainability Guideline* evident in their quality systems, which implies TE Supplement compliance without registration to the Supplement. In any case, the Supplement's requirements affect all TE suppliers, whether they are in the US, Canada, Mexico, Argentina, Australia, Venezuela or any other country.

In some respects, QS-9000, which includes ISO 9001 verbatim within it, parallels the logic applied to medical devices (i.e., ISO 9000 is a series of good generic QMS standards, but it needs additional product- and process-specific requirements to apply to a particular industry).

This move was made by the Big Three in response to suppliers that complained about the expense of developing and maintaining a quality system to meet three sets of different and often competing requirements specified by these OEM customers and a desire by the Big Three to gain some operating efficiencies. Naturally, a primary objective has been to improve quality. This document also has been adopted by a number of truck manufacturers, including

Freightliner, Mack Trucks, Inc., Navistar International Corp., PACCAR, Inc., and Volvo GM Heavy Truck Corp.

The full reach of QS-9000 isn't fully visible, but it is quite interesting. For example, in 1995 the Big Three automakers released *Quality System Requirements QS-9000 Semiconductor Supplement.* The Supplement will become a requirement for all semiconductor companies that supply to members of the Automotive Electronics Council, a cooperative alliance of parts engineering/components engineering and supplier quality groups of Chrysler, Delco Electronics (GM) and Ford. As with QS-9000, the semiconductor document resulted from petitions by the semiconductor industry to create a mutual interpretation and application of the previously individualized company quality system requirements, now standardized in QS-9000.

Finally, law firms that do business with the Big Three automakers are expecting a QS-9000 supplement that will establish quality system requirements for law firms. As with other QS-9000 supplements, the cost of continuing to do business with the automakers may be registration of the law firm to QS-9000. (While several UK law firms are registered to ISO 9001/2, it is uncommon in the United States. Clearly, that will change.)

Summary

The application of ISO 9000—or some variation of ISO 9000 such as QS-9000—in regulated industries involves additional process, product- and/or service-specific requirements. Attorneys will need to understand the basic structure of ISO 9000 and its industry-specific applications to a client in order to provide effective legal counsel.

The application of ISO 9000 to a specific EU new approach directive (e.g., Machinery, Medical Devices, Personal Protective Equipment) will require an in-depth knowledge of that new approach directive and the role of ISO 9000 in that directive. For example, the Technical File in the Machinery Directive can provide excellent product safety information for defense attorneys in the event of a lawsuit. However, the Technical File could also reveal that little was accomplished in conforming to technical standards, because it is a directive where manufacturers self-declare their conformity. Further, examination of the quality system could reveal little in the way of a quality system, because third-party ISO 9001/2/3 registration isn't required. To defend or attack such a Technical File will require a mix of technical mastery of the directive, knowledge of quality systems and a legal appreciation of the significance of EU directives in US product liability lawsuits—they will be very significant in the future.

It will be important to understand the new ISO 9000-driven medical device regulatory structure in the US and EU and in countries adopting similar structures, such as Canada and Australia. This development will continue to grow in significance in medical device regulations and will affect legal practice in those areas. To provide effective legal counsel, it will be necessary to understand the unique character of the quality system and its product-specific medical device safety requirements.

As noted in the text, QS-9000 will provide the area of fastest growth in quality system registrations in the United States. It, too, must be examined with an eye to internal quality system requirements and the product it produces. Since a future QS-9000 supplement likely will impose specific requirements on law firms, it likely will become the best known standard in the legal profession.

Appendix A

ISO 9001

An Overview of the Clauses
...and Their Meaning

1   Scope

This section of ISO 9001 sets forth the intentions and applicability of the standard. The objective is that the standard will become the framework for an organization's quality management system when it incorporates "all stages from design through to servicing." The standard will thus govern how an organization manages its processes to achieve customer satisfaction by preventing nonconformities. ISO 9001 says that the situations to which it is applicable include, "when:

a)   design is required and the product requirements are stated principally in performance terms, or they need to be established, and

b)   confidence in product conformance can be attained by adequate demonstration of a supplier's capabilities in design, development, production, installation and servicing."

2   Normative reference

This section defines the provisions contained within this document (standard) as the provisions of the ISO 9001 International Standard and as the valid and most recent edition at time of publication. This International Standard is subject to revision, and organizations engaged in agreements based on ISO 9001 are encouraged to endeavor to always apply the most recent edition of the standard. This section implies that registration would be lost if an organization were applying an outdated version of ISO 9001 to its QMS. Members of the International Electrotechnical Commission (IEC) and ISO maintain currently valid copies of this and all other International Standards, so they should be conferred with for verification.

As compared with informative references that simply provide guidance, normative references are requirements that must be followed. A specific reference is given to *ISO 8402:1994, Quality management and quality assurance—Vocabulary.*

3   Definitions

This section defines important terms used in the standard: product (3.1), tender (3.2) and contract (3.3).

4   Quality system requirements

This section consists of 20 clauses that outline the required steps and contents that must be included in a QMS in order for an organization's processes to be registered to ISO 9001. These clauses and their subclauses tell you what needs to be done, but they are extremely flexible about how these actions are to be accomplished and what the final system contains. It is up to each organization to decide how effective and productive the QMS will be that it wants to develop and implement.

4.1 Management Responsibility

This clause requires organizations to adopt a QMS using the requirements of Section 4 as its basis and that management take responsibility for the establishing and overseeing of the documentation, implementation and auditing of the QMS.

4.1.1 Quality Policy

This subclause imposes executive responsibility on an organization's management to define and document its quality policy. The policy must be meaningful in meeting both the organization's goals and customer needs and expectations. Management must make sure this policy is "understood, implemented and maintained at all levels of the organization." It is suggested that management establish a quality policy that is brief and easy to implement and understand, so that any employee can remember it, ensure its application to production processes and explain what the policy means rather than recite it verbatim.

Note: ISO 9001 emphasizes the documentation of activities and procedures throughout the 20 clauses. Many of the activities and procedures specified already exist in some form at most organizations— it is simply a matter of putting them in concrete form where they can be reviewed and often improved upon. See Clause 4.5 for more discussion of document and data control.

4.1.2 Organization

This subclause provides guidelines for the systems, personnel and procedures required to organize the quality system.

4.1.2.1 Responsibility and Authority

You must define and document the responsibilities, authority and interrelation of all personnel who affect quality within the organization, especially those employees who need the freedom and authority to:

a) initiate action to prevent the occurrence of any nonconformities relating to the product, process and quality system;

b) identify and record any problems relating to the product, process and quality system;

c) initiate, recommend or provide solutions through designated channels;

d) verify the implementation of solutions;

e) control further processing, delivery or installation of nonconforming product until the deficiency or unsatisfactory condition has been corrected.

Formally defining and documenting employee responsibilities and authorities will allow your organization to evaluate the effectiveness of the present quality control organization and ensure that the system is allowing employees to properly manage quality control.

4.1.2.2 Resources

Executive management is responsible for identifying and then providing the resources necessary to effectively implement and maintain the QMS. This includes the assignment of trained personnel—or the training of personnel—who are capable of managing, performing the work and verifying process quality according to the QMS (see 4.18 for greater discussion of training). The verification activities include internal quality audits.

4.1.2.3 Management Representative

Executive management must appoint one of its own members to serve as a management representative with the authority to:

- Ensure that a QMS is established, implemented and maintained in accordance with the standard.

- Report directly to senior management on the quality system's performance so that senior management can review its performance and take steps to improve the system.

The management representative may also be responsible for interacting externally on issues relating to the QMS—including organizations that set requirements affecting the organization (regulatory bodies and product standards-setting bodies).

Requiring a member of senior management to be responsible for managing the QMS process and for reporting on the system's effectiveness to senior management gives the quality system's role significant weight within the organization. If a high-level manager is the management representative, employees know that he or she has the power to get things done, and they will take this representative as a signal that senior management is fully behind the QMS process. Having a senior management member as the management representative also means that senior management will receive unfiltered reports on QMS processes, problems and results.

4.1.3 Management review

This subclause states that executive management will:

- Review the QMS on a sufficient basis to ensure that the system continues to be suitable and effective in satisfying both ISO 9001's requirements and the organization's quality policy and objectives.

- Maintain records of these reviews (see 4.16 for discussion of record control).

The management representative would be expected to play a significant role in the management review process.

4.2 Quality System

This clause requires an organization to prepare a documented quality system, which involves documenting quality procedures and instructions and effectively implementing them.

4.2.1 General

This subclause states that an organization will prepare a quality manual covering the ISO 9001 requirements and that the manual will "include or make reference to the quality system procedures and outline the structure of the documentation used in the quality system." An advisory note indicates that ISO 10013 offers guidance on quality manuals.

4.2.2 Quality System Procedures

This subclause requires an organization to prepare documented quality system procedures that satisfy the standard's requirements and the organization's quality policy and to implement the QMS and its documented procedures in an effective manner. The range and detail of procedure documentation will depend on the complexity of the work, the methods used and the skills and training personnel require to carry out their work. Documentation should not approach the level of detail required of work instructions, since quality system procedures are meant only to provide a sense of the flow and overall structure to the work environment. An advisory note indicates that you may reference instructions defining the details of how an activity is performed.

4.2.3 Quality planning

This subclause requires an organization to define and document how it will meet its quality requirements. Organizations with fixed product lines will rely more heavily on a quality manual, whereas an organization whose products and services are flexible and vary will depend more on a detailed quality plan.

In either case, an organization is required to do quality planning in a manner that meets the specifications for its products, projects or contracts. This may include:

- Prepare quality plans.

- Identify and acquire any controls, materials, resources and skills needed to achieve the required quality.

- Ensure compatibility of all organizational activities with each other and with applicable documentation.

- Update quality control, inspection and testing techniques as needed.

- Identify measurement requirements exceeding existing capabilities in time to develop capabilities to meet those needs.

- Identify suitable verification methods.

- Clarify standards of acceptability.

- Identify and prepare quality records.

4.3 Contract Review

The clause covers procedures that enable the organization to manage and satisfy its contracts.

4.3.1 General

This subclause states that an organization will have documented procedures for conducting contract review and coordinating related activities.

4.3.2 Review

This subclause requires an organization to review a tender, contract or order prior to submission or acceptance to ensure:

- Adequate definition and documentation of requirements.

- Resolution of differences between the tender requirements and those of the contract or order.

- Organization's ability to meet contract or order requirements.

4.3.3 Amendment to a Contract

This subclause directs the organization to identify how it will amend a contract and how any amendments will be correctly relayed to those functions of the organization affected by changes to that contract.

4.3.4 Records

This subclause indicates that records of contract reviews must be maintained. A note to the subclause suggests that the organization should establish communication channels and interfaces with the customer for the handling of contract matters.

4.4 Design Control

This clause does not appear in ISO 9002 and applies only to an organization that is design responsible.

4.4.1 General

This subclause states that an organization must establish and maintain documented procedures that will control and verify product design to ensure the product meets its specified requirements.

4.4.2 Design and Development Planning

This subclause states that an organization will prepare plans for each design and development activity. It specifies that the plans define who is responsible for their implementation and that the responsible parties are qualified and equipped with the resources to effectively accomplish the design and development activities. Design plans must be updated if the design changes.

4.4.3 Organizational and Technical Interfaces

A number of different groups within an organization may provide input into the design process for a given product, and this subclause requires that organizational and technical interfaces among these groups be defined and that pertinent information related to the interfaces be "documented, transmitted and regularly reviewed."

4.4.4 Design Input

This subclause directs the organization to do the following for a given product:

- Identify and document design input requirements.

- Review the adequacy of the requirements.

- Ensure that the requirements are complete and that any ambiguities or conflicts among the requirements are resolved.

This process includes applicable statutory and regulatory requirements, and it must take contract review activities into account.

4.4.5 Design Output

Design outputs are technical documents related to production and servicing activities, including drawings, specifications, instructions, software and servicing procedures. This subclause provides that design output must be "documented and expressed in terms that can be verified and validated against design input requirements." Design output must:

- Meet design input requirements.

- Contain or make reference to acceptance criteria.

- Identify design characteristics critical to the safe and proper functioning of the product.

- Provide for design output document review before product release.

4.4.6 Design Review

This subclause mandates that the organization plan and conduct "formal documented reviews" of the design results at appropriate points in the design process. Representatives of all functions relevant to the stage of design being reviewed, as well as other specialists as required, must participate in each design review. Records of these reviews must be maintained. Ultimately, senior management and those involved in the design functions of the organization have the discretion to decide when these reviews are necessary and useful and how broad participation will be beyond representatives of those departments affecting—and affected by—the design aspects of the product or service under review.

4.4.7 Design Verification

This subclause states that design verification will be performed at appropriate points in the design process to ensure that design stage output meets input requirements. The organization is required to record which measures are being used to conduct design verification.

A note suggests that an organization might consider the following activities in addition to design review to achieve design verification:

● Perform alternative calculations.

● Compare the new design with a similar, proven design.

● Test and perform demonstrations.

● Review the design stage documents before release.

4.4.8 Design Validation

While design verification ensures that the design process meets design input requirements, this subclause requires design validation to ensure the product satisfies defined user needs and/or requirements.

A series of notes provides the following information:

● Validation should follow successful verification.

● Operating conditions should meet defined parameters when conducting validation.

● Validation may be necessary at stages prior to product completion.

● If the product is intended to serve different uses for different customers, multiple validations may be necessary.

4.4.9 Design Changes

This subclause specifies that all changes and modifications to a design must be "identified, documented, reviewed and approved by authorized personnel before their implementation." Many factors can require design changes, and changes to designs are a normal part of many product and service operations. The purpose here is to control the process of change to ensure efficiency, accuracy and consistency.

4.5 Document and Data Control

Clause 4.5 covers procedures to control documents, an important aspect of an ISO 9001-based quality system.

4.5.1 General

This subclause requires an organization to establish and maintain documented procedures to control documents and data relevant to the quality system, including external documents (customer-supplied materials and applicable standards).

4.5.2 Document and Data Approval and Issue

Before being issued, all documents and data must be reviewed and approved for adequacy. Companies must also establish and make available a master list or similar procedure to ensure that current revisions of documents are used and controlled.

4.5.3 Document and Data Changes

This subclause requires an organization to give responsibility for review and approval of changes to controlled documents/data to those individuals and groups that undertook the original review and approval. They are to be provided with the necessary information to effectively review and approve the change, and changes to documents and data are to be noted in the document or in attachments where possible.

4.6 Purchasing

4.6.1 General

This subclause requires an organization to establish documented procedures to ensure that its suppliers supply products of the required quality to satisfy the organization's customer needs.

4.6.2 Evaluation of Subcontractors

The "supplier" will:

- Evaluate and choose subcontractors based on their ability to meet the supplier's requirements.

- Define the type and extent of its control over subcontractors.

- Establish and maintain records for acceptable subcontractors.

4.6.3 Purchasing Data

Purchasing documents will clearly contain information describing the product ordered, including:

- A precise form of identification (e.g., type, class, grade)

- Other means of product identification, as well as specifications, drawings, process requirements, inspection instructions and other relevant data (e.g., requirements for approval or qualification of product, procedures, process equipment and personnel)

- Information on any quality system standard applicable to the product.

Prior to release, the organization will review and approve the information detailed on the purchasing document.

4.6.4 Verification of Purchased Product

This subclause applies to verification at a supplier's facility by the organization or its customer.

4.6.4.1 Supplier Verification of Subcontractor's Premises

The purchasing orders must specify the arrangements the organization requires to verify the quality of purchased product at its supplier's facilities, if verification is required.

4.6.4.2 Customer Verification of Subcontracted Product

If specified in the contract, the customer or customer's representative can verify the product's conformity to specifications at its subcontractor's and/or supplier's premises. This subclause states that the organization is still responsible for providing acceptable product to the customer.

4.7 Control of Customer-Supplied Product

This clause requires documented procedures for the control of products supplied by a customer for incorporation into the product to be supplied to the customer. The organization is responsible for proper handling and maintenance of customer-supplied product, and any product that becomes unsuitable for use must be documented and reported to the customer.

4.8 Product Identification and Traceability

This clause requires, where applicable, documented procedures to enable the organization to identify product from receipt through production to installation. The organization must also provide the means to trace individual pieces and batches of the product to the degree specified by the customer contract.

4.9 Process Control

The organization is required to:

- Identify and plan the procedures to be used in manufacturing, installing and servicing the product.

- Ensure that these processes are carried out under controlled conditions.

- Provide documented instructions for work that affects quality.

- Monitor and approve necessary processes.

- Specify relevant criteria for workmanship.

- Ensure continuing process capability through proper equipment maintenance.

- Validate the process, determine equipment capability and certify personnel for special processes.

4.10 Inspection and Testing

This clause covers aspects of the inspection and testing required to ensure product quality meets customer specifications, from delivery of product and materials to the organization through final inspection of product being supplied to the customer.

4.10.1 General

This subclause requires the organization to determine what procedures are necessary for inspection and testing activities and to document those procedures to ensure product requirements are met.

4.10.2 Receiving Inspection and Testing

This subclause requires the organization to perform necessary inspection and testing on product supplied by its suppliers.

4.10.2.1

To verify that its supplier is fulfilling its contractual requirements, the organization is required to:

- Inspect or otherwise verify incoming product before use.

- Verify the product conforms to specified requirements — the quality plan or documented procedures.

4.10.2.2

Consideration is required of the amount of control exercised by the organization at its supplier's premises and the documented evidence of specification conformance provided.

4.10.2.3

The organization must positively identify and record incoming products released for urgent production, in case recall and replacement becomes necessary due to nonconformities.

4.10.3 In-Process Inspection and Testing

This clause requires the organization to inspect and test the product as required by the quality plan or documented procedures. Product must be held until all tests have been completed unless positive recall procedures discussed in 4.10.2.3 are followed.

4.10.4 Final Inspection and Testing

The organization will not release product from its facility until every activity specified within the quality plan and/or document procedures are completed. This subclause requires verification of all testing and inspection activities during the production cycle.

4.10.5 Inspection and Test Records

This subclause requires the organization to establish and maintain records that indicate whether a product has passed or failed specified tests and inspections. A product that fails any test or inspection requirement should be handled under the procedures for control of nonconforming product (see 4.13).

4.11 Control of Inspection, Measuring and Test Equipment

This clause requires an organization to maintain the accuracy of the methods used to inspect, measure and test product and system elements.

4.11.1 General

This subclause requires the organization to establish and maintain documented procedures for the control, calibration and maintenance of inspection, measuring and test equipment to verify the product meets specified requirements. Procedures are required to:

- Ensure use of this equipment produces consistent results that fall within acceptable variability ranges.

- Regularly verify and document the ability of test software and hardware used for inspection purposes.

- Make available to the customer, when required, technical data that verifies the adequacy of the controls on the equipment.

4.11.2 Control Procedure

This subclause provides details of the necessities for testing accuracy, calibration of equipment, handling of equipment and documentation of the checking procedures.

4.12 Inspection and Test Status

This clause requires the organization to identify conforming and nonconforming product by maintaining procedures that identify the product's inspection and test status throughout the production cycle. In other words, you should be able to identify product status at any stage of the production process.

4.13 Control of Nonconforming Product

4.13.1 General

This subclause requires the supplier to establish and maintain guidelines to prevent the inadvertent use or installation of nonconforming products, including identification, documentation, evaluation, segregation, disposal and notification of relevant parties.

4.13.2 Review and Disposition of Nonconforming Product

This subclause requires the clarification of who is responsible for review and disposition of nonconforming product and to document the disposition of the product. The organization must follow documented procedures for review of nonconforming product to decide if it should be reworked, accepted by the customer with or without repair, reworked for alternate use or scrapped.

4.14 Corrective and Preventive Action

This clause covers corrective action to eliminate an existing nonconformity and preventive action to prevent a potential nonconformity in the first place.

4.14.1 General

This subclause requires the organization to establish and maintain documented corrective and preventive action strategies proportionate to the severity of problems and the potential risks being addressed.

4.14.2 Corrective action

Procedures for corrective action must define:

- How customer complaints and nonconformity reports are to be handled.

- What to investigate and analyze to determine the problem and then to record the results.

- What corrective action is needed to eliminate a cause of nonconformities.

- How controls are to be applied to ensure that corrective actions taken are effective.

4.14.3 Preventive Action

This subclause requires the organization to utilize all available documentation and data to detect, analyze and remove potential causes of nonconformities. Once a cause is identified, the supplier must determine a method of preventive action, initiate that method and submit relevant information on actions taken to management.

4.15 Handling, Storage, Packaging, Preservation and Delivery

Under this clause, the organization must establish and maintain documented procedures for controlling products during these stages and develop guidelines to:

- Develop a damage-prevention scheme.

- Provide for secure storage.

- Control packaging, packing and marking processes.

- Make sure products aren't inadvertently destroyed or misplaced.

- Provide for ultimate safe delivery to customer after final inspection and test.

4.15.1 General

This subclause requires the organization to establish and maintain documented procedures.

4.15.2 Handling

This subclause requires development of procedures to protect product from damage or deterioration at all stages of the production cycle.

4.15.3 Storage

This subclause requires the organization to designate storage locations for product to protect it from receipt to delivery. This includes regular inspections during storage to ensure maintenance of product quality.

4.15.4 Packaging

This subclause requires the organization to control packing, packaging and marking processes to satisfy quality requirements.

4.15.5 Preservation

This subclause requires the organization to establish methods to maintain the efficacy of product during the organization's possession.

4.15.6 Delivery

This subclause requires the organization to maintain procedures to ensure product quality after final inspection and test.

4.16 Control of Quality Records

This clause requires the organization to establish and maintain controls for quality records that document conformance of products to specified customer requirements and the effective operation of the quality system. Records are not restricted to printed hard copies, they can be electronic. Records must be legible and held for a specified period of time.

4.17 Internal Quality Audits

This clause requires the organization to conduct internal audits to verify that the quality system implemented is operating in compliance with ISO 9001 and meets the quality needs of the customer. Audit results will be documented and those responsible for that specified area must be informed of the results.

Those responsible must make timely corrections so that the quality system once again falls in line with what is required. A follow-up audit is required to verify and record implementation and effectiveness of corrective actions. Internal audit team members can't audit their own work areas.

4.18 Training

This clause requires the organization to identify training needs, train all personnel that affect quality and maintain records of this training.

4.19 Servicing

If servicing (after sales servicing) is specified, this clause requires documented procedures to be in place to effectively perform servicing, and the organization must follow these procedures.

4.20 Statistical Techniques

This clause requires the organization to develop a system to make certain proper statistical techniques are used to ensure products satisfy customer needs.

4.20.1 Identification of Need

This subclause requires the organization to identify those statistical techniques required to ensure quality in all stages of the production cycle (process capability and product characteristics).

4.20.2 Procedures

This subclause requires the organization to have documented procedures to implement and control those statistical techniques identified as necessary for quality in the production cycle.

Appendix B — EU Directive

The Product Liability Directive

COUNCIL DIRECTIVE of 25 July 1985

on the approximation of the laws, regulations and administrative provisions of the Member States concerning liability for defective products

(85/374/EEC)

THE COUNCIL OF THE EUROPEAN COMMUNITIES,

Having regard to the Treaty establishing the European Economic Community, and in particular Article 100 thereof,

Having regard to the proposal from the Commission[1],

Having regard to the opinion of the European Parliament[2],

Having regard to the opinion of the Economic and Social Committee[3],

Whereas approximation of the laws of the Member States concerning the liability of the producer for damage caused by the defectiveness of his products is necessary because the existing divergences may distort competition and affect the movement of goods within the common market and entail a differing degree of protection of the consumer against damage caused by a defective product to his health or property;

Whereas liability without fault on the part of the producer is the sole means of adequately solving the problem, peculiar to our age of increasing technicality, of a fair apportionment of the risks inherent in modern technological production;

Whereas liability without fault should apply only to movables which have been industrially produced; whereas, as a result, it is appropriate to exclude liability for agricultural products and game, except where they have undergone a processing of an industrial nature which could cause a defect in these products; whereas the liability provided for in this Directive should also apply to movables which are used in the construction of immovables or are installed in immovables;

Whereas protection of the consumer requires that all producers involved in the production process should be made liable, in so far as their finished product, component part or any raw material supplied by them was defective; whereas, for the same reason, liability should extend to importers of products into the Community and to persons who present themselves as producers by affixing their name, trade mark or other distinguishing feature or who supply a product the producer of which cannot be identified;

Whereas, in situations where several persons are liable for the same damage, the protection of the consumer requires that the injured person should be able to claim full compensation for the damage from any one of them;

Whereas, to protect the physical well-being and property of the consumer, the defectiveness of the product should be determined by reference not to its fitness for use but to the lack of the safety which the public at large is entitled to expect; whereas the safety is assessed by excluding any misuse of the product not reasonable under the circumstances;

Whereas a fair apportionment of risk between the injured person and the producer implies that the producer should be able to free himself from liability if he furnishes proof as to the existence of certain exonerating circumstances;

Whereas the protection of the consumer requires that the liability of the producer remains unaffected by acts or omissions of other persons having contributed to cause the damage; whereas, however, the contributory negligence of the injured person may be taken into account to reduce or disallow such liability;

Whereas the protection of the consumer requires compensation for death and personal injury as well as compensation for damage to property; whereas the latter should nevertheless be limited to goods for private use or consumption and be subject to a deduction of a lower threshold of a fixed amount in order to avoid litigation in an excessive number of cases; whereas this Directive should not prejudice compensation for pain and suffering and other non-material damages payable, where appropriate, under the law applicable to the case;

Whereas a uniform period of limitation for the bringing of action for compensation is in the interests both of the injured person and of the producer;

Whereas products age in the course of time, higher safety standards are developed and the state of science and technology progresses; whereas, therefore, it would not be reasonable to make the producer liable for an unlimited period for the defectiveness of his product; whereas, therefore, liability should expire after a reasonable length of time, without prejudice to claims pending at law;

Whereas, to achieve effective protection of consumers, no contractual derogation should be permitted as regards the liability of the producer in relation to the injured person;

Whereas under the legal systems of the Member States an injured party may have a claim for damages based on grounds of contractual liability or on grounds of non-contractual liability other than that provided for in this Directive; in so far as these provisions also serve to attain the objective of effective protection of consumers, they should remain unaffected by this Directive; whereas, in so far as effective protection of consumers in the sector of pharmaceutical products is already also attained in a Member State under a special liability system, claims based on this system should similarly remain possible;

Whereas, to the extent that liability for nuclear injury or damage is already covered in all Member States by adequate special rules, it has been possible to exclude damage of this type from the scope of this Directive;

Whereas, since the exclusion of primary agricultural products and game from the scope of this Directive may be felt, in certain Member States, in view of what is expected for the protection of consumers, to restrict unduly such protection, it should be possible for a Member State to extend liability to such products;

Whereas, for similar reasons, the possibility offered to a producer to free himself from liability if he proves that the state of scientific and technical knowledge at the time when he put the product into circulation was not such as to enable the existence of a defect to be discovered may be felt in certain Member States to restrict unduly the protection of the consumer; whereas it should therefore be possible for a Member State to maintain in its legislation or to provide by new legislation that this exonerating circumstance is not admitted; whereas, in the case of new legislation, making use of this derogation should, however, be subject to a Community stand-still procedure, in order to raise, if possible, the level of protection in a uniform manner throughout the Community;

Whereas, taking into account the legal traditions in most of the Member States, it is inappropriate to set any financial ceiling on the producer's liability without fault; whereas, in so far as there are, however, differing traditions, it seems possible to admit that a Member State may derogate from the principle of unlimited liability by providing a limit for the total liability of the producer for damage resulting from a death or personal injury and caused by identical items with the same defect, provided that this limit is established at a level sufficiently high to guarantee adequate protection of the consumer and the correct functioning of the common market;

Whereas the harmonization resulting from this cannot be total at the present stage, but opens the way towards greater harmonization; whereas it is therefore necessary that the Council receive at regular intervals, reports from the Commission on the application of this Directive, accompanied, as the case may be, by appropriate proposals;

Whereas it is particularly important in this respect that a re-examination be carried out of those parts of the Directive relating to the derogations open to the Member States, at the expiry of a period of sufficient length to gather practical experience on the effects of these derogations on the protection of consumers and on the functioning of the common market,

HAS ADOPTED THIS DIRECTIVE:

Article I

The producer shall be liable for damage caused by a defect in his product.

Article 2

For the purpose of this Directive 'product' means all movables, with the exception of primary agricultural products and game, even though incorporated into another movable or into an immovable. 'Primary agricultural products' means the products of the soil, of stock-farming and of fisheries, excluding products which have undergone initial processing. 'Product' includes electricity.

Article 3

1. 'Producer' means the manufacturer of a finished product, the producer of any raw material or the manufacturer of a component part and any person who, by putting his name, trade mark or other distinguishing feature on the product presents himself as its producer.

2. Without prejudice to the liability of the producer, any person who imports into the Community a product for sale, hire, leasing or any form of distribution in the course of his business shall be deemed to be a producer within the meaning of this Directive and shall be responsible as a producer.

3. Where the producer of the product cannot be identified, each supplier of the product shall be treated as its producer unless he informs the injured person, within a reasonable time, of the identity of the producer or of the person who supplied him with the product. The same shall apply, in the case of an imported product, if this product does not indicate the identity of the importer referred to in paragraph 2, even if the name of the producer is indicated.

Article 4

The injured person shall be required to prove the damage, the defect and the causal relationship between defect and damage.

Article 5

Where, as a result of the provisions of this Directive, two or more persons are liable for the same damage, they shall be liable jointly and severally, without prejudice to the provisions of national law concerning the rights of contribution or recourse.

Article 6

1. A product is defective when it does not provide the safety which a person is entitled to expect, taking all circumstances into account, including:

(a) the presentation of the product;

(b) the use to which it could reasonably be expected that the product would be put;

(c) the time when the product was put into circulation.

2. A product shall not be considered defective for the sole reason that a better product is subsequently put into circulation.

Article 7

The producer shall not be liable as a result of this Directive if he proves:

(a) that he did not put the product into circulation; or

(b) that, having regard to the circumstances, it is probable that the defect which caused the damage did not exist at the time when the product was put into circulation by him or that this defect came into being afterwards; or

(c) that the product was neither manufactured by him for sale or any form of distribution for economic purpose nor manufactured or distributed by him in the course of his business; or

(d) that the defect is due to compliance of the product with mandatory regulations issued by the public authorities; or

(e) that the state of scientific and technical knowledge at the time when he put the product into circulation was not such as to enable the existence of the defect to be discovered; or

(f) in the case of a manufacturer of a component, that the defect is attributable to the design of the product in which the component has been fitted or to the instructions given by the manufacturer of the product.

Article 8

1. Without prejudice to the provisions of national law concerning the right of contribution or recourse, the liability of the producer shall not be reduced when the damage is caused both by a defect in

product and by the act or omission of a third party.

2. The liability of the producer may be reduced or disallowed when, having regard to all the circumstances, the damage is caused both by a defect in the product and by the fault of the injured person or any person for whom the injured person is responsible.

Article 9

For the purpose of Article 1, 'damage' means:

(a) damage caused by death or by personal injuries;

(b) damage to, or destruction of, any item of property other than the defective product itself, with a lower threshold of 500 ECU, provided that the item of property:

   (i) is of a type ordinarily intended for private use or consumption, and

   (ii) was used by the injured person mainly for his own private use or consumption.

This Article shall be without prejudice to national provisions relating to non-material damage.

Article 10

1. Member States shall provide in their legislation that a limitation period of three years shall apply to proceedings for the recovery of damages as provided for in this Directive. The limitation period shall begin to run from the day on which the plaintiff became aware, or should reasonably have become aware, of the damage, the defect and the identity of the producer.

2. The laws of Member States regulating suspension or interruption of the limitation period shall not be affected by this Directive.

Article 11

Member States shall provide in their legislation that the rights conferred upon the injured person pursuant to this Directive shall be extinguished upon the expiry of a period of 10 years from the date on which the producer put into circulation the actual product which caused the damage, unless the injured person has in the meantime instituted proceedings against the producer.

Article 12

The liability of the producer arising from this Directive may not, in relation to the injured person, be limited or excluded by a provision limiting his liability or exempting him from liability.

Article 13

This Directive shall not affect any rights which an injured person may have according to the rules of the law of contractual or non-contractual liability or a special liability system existing at the moment when this Directive is notified.

Article 14

This Directive shall not apply to injury or damage arising from nuclear accidents and covered by international conventions ratified by the Member States.

Article 15

1. Each Member State may:

(a) by way of derogation from Article 2, provide in its legislation that within the meaning of Article I of this Directive 'product' also means primary agricultural products and game;

(b) by way of derogation from Article 7 (e), maintain or, subject to the procedure set out in paragraph 2 of this Article, provide in this legislation that the producer shall be liable even if he proves that the state of scientific and technical knowledge at the time when he put the product into circulation was not such as to enable the existence of a defect to be discovered.

2. A Member State wishing to introduce the measure specified in paragraph I (b) shall communicate the text of the proposed measure to the Commission. The Commission shall inform the other Member States thereof.

The Member State concerned shall hold the proposed measure in abeyance for nine months after the Commission is informed and provided that in the meantime the Commission has not submitted to the Council a proposal amending this Directive on the relevant matter. However, if within three months of receiving the said information, the Commission does not advise the Member State concerned that it intends submitting such a proposal to the Council, the Member State may take the proposed measure immediately.

If the Commission does submit to the Council such a proposal amending this Directive within the aforementioned nine months, the Member State concerned shall hold the proposed measure in abeyance for a further period of 18 months from the date on which the proposal is submitted.

3. Ten years after the date of notification of this Directive, the Commission shall submit to the Council a report on the effect that rulings by the courts as to the application of Article 7 (e) and of paragraph I (b) of this Article have on consumer protection and the functioning of the common market. In the light of this report the Council, acting on a proposal from the Commission and pursuant to the terms of Article 100 of the Treaty, shall decide whether to repeal Article 7 (e).

Article 16

1. Any Member State may provide that a producer's total liability for damage resulting from a death or personal injury and caused by identical items with the same defect shall be limited to an amount which may not be less than 70 million ECU.

2. Ten years after the date of notification of this Directive, the Commission shall submit to the Council a report on the effect on consumer protection and the functioning of the common market of the implementation of the financial limit on liability by those Member States which have used the option provided for in paragraph 1. In the light of this report the Council, acting on a proposal from the Commission and pursuant to the terms of Article 100 of the Treaty, shall decide whether to repeal paragraph 1.

Article 17

This Directive shall not apply to products put into circulation before the date on which the provisions referred to in Article 19 enter into force.

Article 18

1. For the purposes of this Directive, the ECU shall be that defined

by Regulation (EEC) No 3180/78[4] , as amended by Regulation (EEC) No 2626/84[5] , The equivalent in national currency shall initially be calculated at the rate obtaining on the date of adoption of this Directive.

2. Every five years the Council, acting on a proposal from the Commission, shall examine and, if need be, revise the amounts in this Directive, in the light of economic and monetary trends in the Community.

Article 19

1. Member States shall bring into force, not later than three years from the date of notification of this Directive, the laws, regulations and administrative provisions necessary to comply with this Directive. They shall forthwith inform the Commission thereof[6] .

2. The procedure set out in Article I5 (2) shall apply from the date of notification of this Directive.

Article 20

Member States shall communicate to the Commission the texts of the main provisions of national law which they subsequently adopt in the field governed by this Directive.

Article 21

Every five years the Commission shall present a report to the Council on the application of this Directive and, if necessary, shall submit appropriate proposals to it.

Article 22

This Directive is addressed to the Member States.

Done at Brussels, 25 July 1985.

For the Council

The President

J. POOS

ENDNOTES

[1] OJ No C 241, 14. 10. 1976, p. 9 and OJ No C 271, 26. 10. 1979, p. 3.

[2] OJ No C 127, 21. 5. 1979, p. 61.

[3] OJ No C 114, 7. 5. 1979, p. 15.

[4] OJ No L 379, 30. 12. 1978, p. 1.

[5] OJ No L 247, 16. 9. 1984, p. 1.

[6] This Directive was notified to the Member States on 30 July 1985.

Appendix C — EU Directive

The Product Safety Directive

Council Directive 92/59/EEC of 29 June 1992 on General Product Safety

THE COUNCIL OF THE EUROPEAN COMMUNITIES,

Having regard to the Treaty establishing the European Economic Community, and in particular Article 100a thereof,

Having regard to the proposal from the Commission[1],

In cooperation with the European Parliament[2],

Having regard to the opinion of the Economic and Social Committee[3],

Whereas it is important to adopt measures with the aim of progressively establishing the internal market over a period expiring on 31 December 1992; whereas the internal market is to comprise an area without internal frontiers in which the free movement of goods, persons, services and capital is ensured;

Whereas some Member States have adopted horizontal legislation on product safety, imposing, in particular, a general obligation on economic operators to market only safe products; whereas those legislations differ in the level of protection afforded to persons; whereas such disparities and the absence of horizontal legislation in other Member States are liable to create barriers to trade and distortions of competition within the internal market;

Whereas it is very difficult to adopt Community legislation for every product which exists or may be developed; whereas there is a need for a broadly-based, legislative framework of a horizontal nature to deal with those products, and also to cover lacunae in existing or forthcoming specific legislation, in particular with a view to ensuring a high level of protection of safety and health of persons, as required by Article 100 a (3) of the Treaty;

Whereas it is therefore necessary to establish on a Community level a general safety requirement for any product placed on the market that is intended for consumers or likely to be used by consumers; whereas certain second-hand goods should nevertheless be excluded by their nature;

Whereas production equipment, capital goods and other products used exclusively in the context of a trade or business are not covered by this Directive;

Whereas, in the absence of more specific safety provisions, within the frame work of Community regulations, covering the products concerned, the provisions of this Directive are to apply;

Whereas when there are specific rules of Community law, of the total harmonization type, and in particular rules adopted on the basis of the new approach, which lay down obligations regarding product safety, further obligations should not be imposed on economic operators as regards the placing on the market of products covered by such rules;

Whereas, when the provisions of specific Community regulations cover only certain aspects of safety or categories of risks in respect of the product concerned, the obligations of economic operators in respect of such aspects are determined solely by those provisions;

Whereas it is appropriate to supplement the duty to observe the general safety requirement by an obligation on economic operators to supply consumers with relevant information and adopt measures commensurate with the characteristics of the products, enabling them to be informed of the risks that these products might present;

Whereas in the absence of specific regulations, criteria should be defined whereby product safety can be assessed;

Whereas Member States must establish authorities responsible for monitoring product safety and with powers to take the appropriate measures;

Whereas it is necessary in particular for the appropriate measures to include the power for Member States to organize, immediately and efficiently, the withdrawal of dangerous products already placed on the market;

Whereas it is necessary for the preservation of the unity of the market to inform the Commission of any measure restricting the placing on the market of a product or requiring its withdrawal from the market except for those relating to an event which is local in effect and in any case limited to the territory of the Member State concerned; whereas such measures can be taken only in compliance with the provisions of the Treaty, and in particular Articles 30 to 36;

Whereas this Directive applies without prejudice to the notification procedures in Council Directive 83/189/EEC of 28 March 1983 laying down a procedure for the provision of information in the field of technical standards and regulations[4] and in Commission Decision 88/383/EEC of 24 February 1988 providing for the improvement of information on safety, hygiene and health at work[5];

Whereas effective supervision of product safety requires the setting-up at national and Community levels of a system of rapid exchange of information in emergency situations in respect of the safety of a product and whereas the procedure laid down by Council Decision 89/45/EEC of 21 December 1988 on a Community system for the rapid exchange of information on dangers arising from the use of consumer products[6] should therefore be incorporated into this Directive and the above Decision should be repealed; whereas it is also advisable for this Directive to take over the detailed procedures adopted under the above Decision and to give the Commission, assisted by a committee, power to adapt them;

Whereas, moreover, equivalent notification procedures already exist for pharmaceuticals, which come under Directives 75/319/EEC[7] and 81/851/EEC[8], concerning animal diseases referred to in Directive 82/894/EEC[9], for products of animal origin covered by Directive 89/662/EEC[10], and in the form of the system for the rapid exchange of information in radiological emergencies under Decision 87/600/Euratom[11];

Whereas it is primarily for Member States, in compliance with the Treaty and in particular with Articles 30 to 36 thereof, to take appropriate measures with regard to dangerous products located within their territory;

Whereas in such a situation the decision taken on a particular product could differ from one Member State to another; whereas such a difference may entail unacceptable disparities in consumer protection and constitute a barrier to intra-Community trade;

Whereas it may be necessary to cope with serious product-safety problems which affect or could affect, in the immediate future, all or a large part of the Community and which, in view of the nature of the safety problem posed by the product cannot be dealt with effectively in a manner commensurate with the urgency of the problem under the procedures laid down in the specific rules of Community law applicable to the products or category of products in question;

Whereas it is therefore necessary to provide for an adequate mechanism allowing, in the last resort, for the adoption of measures applicable throughout the Community, in the form of a decision addressed to the Member States, in order to cope with emergency situations as mentioned above; whereas such a decision is not of direct application to economic operators and must be incorporated into a national instrument; whereas measures adopted under such a procedure can be no more than interim measures that have to be taken by the Commission assisted by a committee of representatives of the Member States; whereas, for reasons of cooperation with the Member States, it is appropriate to provide for a regulatory committee according to procedure III (b) of Decision 87/373/EEC[12];

Whereas this Directive does not affect victims' rights within the meaning of Council Directive 85/374/EEC of 25 July 1985 on the approximation of the laws, regulations and administrative provisions of the Member States concerning liability for defective products[13];

Whereas it is necessary that Member States provide for appropriate means of redress before the competent courts in respect of measures taken by the competent authorities which restrict the placing on the market of a product or require its withdrawal;

Whereas it is appropriate to consider, in the light of experience, possible adaptation of this Directive, particularly as regards extension of its scope and provisions on emergency situations and intervention at Community level;

Whereas, in addition, the adoption of measures concerning imported products with a view to preventing risks to the safety and health of persons must comply with the Community's international obligations,

HAS ADOPTED THIS DIRECTIVE:

TITLE I
Objective—Scope—Definitions

Article 1

1. The purpose of the provisions of this Directive is to ensure that products placed on the market are safe.

2. The provisions of this Directive shall apply in so far as there are no specific provisions in rules of Community law governing the safety of the products concerned.

In particular, where specific rules of Community law contain provisions imposing safety requirements on the products which they govern, the provisions of Articles 2 to 4 of this Directives hall not, in any event, apply to those products.

Where specific rules of Community law contain provisions governing only certain aspects of product safety or categories of risks for the products concerned, those are the provisions which shall apply to the products concerned with regard to the relevant safety aspects or risks.

Article 2

For the purposes of this Directive:

(a) *product* shall mean any product intended for consumers or likely to be used by consumers, supplied whether for consideration or not in the course of a commercial activity and whether new, used or reconditioned.

However, this Directive shall not apply to second-hand products supplied as antiques or as products to be repaired or reconditioned prior to being used, provided that the supplier clearly informs the person to whom he supplies the product to that effect;

(b) *safe product* shall mean any product which, under normal or reasonably foreseeable conditions of use, including duration, does not present any risk or only the minimum risks compatible with the product's use, considered as acceptable and consistent with a high level of protection for the safety and health of persons, taking into account the following points in particular:

- the characteristics of the product, including its composition, packaging, instructions for assembly and maintenance,

- the effect on other products, where it is reasonably foreseeable that it will be used with other products,

- the presentation of the product, the labelling, any instructions for its use and disposal and any other indication or information provided by the producer,

- the categories of consumers at serious risk when using the product, in particular children.

The feasibility of obtaining higher levels of safety or the availability of other products presenting a lesser degree of risk shall not constitute grounds for considering a product to be 'unsafe' or 'dangerous';

(c) *dangerous product* shall mean any product which does not meet the definition of 'safe product' according to point (b) hereof;

(d) *producer* shall mean:

- the manufacturer of the product, when he is established in the Community, and any other person presenting himself as the manufacturer by affixing to the product his name, trademark or other distinctive mark, or the person who reconditions the product,

- the manufacturer's representative, when the manufacturer is not established in the Community or, if there is no representative established in the Community, the importer of the product,

- other professionals in the supply chain, insofar as their activities may affect the safety properties of a product placed on the market.

(e) *distributor* shall mean any professional in the supply chain whose activity does not affect the safety properties of a product.

TITLE II
General safety requirement

Article 3

1. Producers shall be obliged to place only safe products on the market.

2. Within the limits of their respective activities, producers shall:

- provide consumers with the relevant information to enable them to assess the risks inherent in a product throughout the normal or reasonably foreseeable period of its use, where such risks are not immediately obvious without adequate warnings, and to take precautions against those risks.

Provision of such warnings does not, however, exempt any person from compliance with the other requirements laid down in this Directive,

- adopt measures commensurate with the characteristics of the products which they supply, to enable them to be informed of risks which these products might present and to take appropriate action including, if necessary, withdrawing the product in question from the market to avoid these risks.

The above measures shall for example include, whenever appropriate, marking of the products or product batches in such a way that they can be identified, sample testing of marketed products, investigating complaints made and keeping distributors informed of such monitoring.

3. Distributors shall be required to act with due care in order to help to ensure compliance with the general safety requirement, in

particular by not supplying products which they know or should have presumed, on the basis of the information in their possession and as professionals, do not comply with this requirement. In particular, within the limits of their respective activities, they shall participate in monitoring the safety of products placed on the market, especially by passing on information on product risks and cooperating in the action taken to avoid these risks.

Article 4

1. Where there are no specific Community provisions governing the safety of the products in question, a product shall be deemed safe when it conforms to the specific rules of national law of the Member State in whose territory the product is in circulation, such rules being drawn up in conformity with the Treaty, and in particular Articles 30 and 36 thereof, and laying down the health and safety requirements which the product must satisfy in order to be marketed.

2. In the absence of specific rules as referred to in paragraph 1, the conformity of a product to the general safety requirement shall be assessed having regard to voluntary national standards giving effect to a European standard or, where they exist, to Community technical specifications or, failing these, to standards drawn up in the Member State in which the product is in circulation, or to the codes of good practice in respect of health and safety in the sector concerned or to the state of the art and technology and to the safety which consumers may reasonably expect.

3. Conformity of a product with the provisions mentioned in paragraphs 1 or 2 shall not bar the competent authorities of the Member States from taking appropriate measures to impose restrictions on its being placed on the market or to require its withdrawal from the market where there is evidence that, despite such conformity, it is dangerous to the health and safety of consumers.

Title III
Obligations and powers of the Member States

Article 5

Member States shall adopt the necessary laws, regulations and administrative provisions to make producers and distributors comply with their obligations under this Directive in such a way that products placed on the market are safe.

In particular, Member States shall establish or nominate authorities to monitor the compliance of products with the obligation to place only safe products on the market and arrange for such authorities to have the necessary powers to take the appropriate measures incumbent upon them under this Directive, including the possibility of imposing suitable penalties in the event of failure to comply with the obligations deriving from this Directive. They shall notify the Commission of the said authorities; the Commission shall pass on the information to the other Member States.

Article 6

1. For the purposes of Article 5, Member States shall have the necessary powers, acting in accordance with the degree or risk and in conformity with the Treaty, and in particular Articles 30 and 36 thereof, to adopt appropriate measures with a view, *inter alia*, to:

(a) organizing appropriate checks on the safety properties of products, even after their being placed on the market as being safe, on an adequate scale, up to the final stage of use or consumption;

(b) requiring all necessary information from the parties concerned;

(c) taking samples of a product or a product line and subjecting them to safety checks;

(d) subjecting product marketing to prior conditions designed to ensure product safety and requiring that suitable warnings be affixed regarding the risks which the product may present;

(e) making arrangements to ensure that persons who might be exposed to a risk from a product are informed in good time and in a suitable manner of the said risk by, *inter alia*, the publication of special warnings;

(f) temporarily prohibiting, for the period required to carry out the various checks, anyone from supplying, offering to supply or exhibiting a product or product batch, whenever there are precise and consistent indications that they are dangerous;

(g) prohibiting the placing on the market of a product or product batch which has proved dangerous and establishing the accompanying measures needed to ensure that the ban is complied with;

(h) organizing the effective and immediate withdrawal of a dangerous product or product batch already on the market and, if necessary, its destruction under appropriate conditions.

2. The measures to be taken by the competent authorities of the Member States under this Article shall be addressed, as appropriate, to:

(a) the producer;

(b) within the limits of their respective activities, distributors and in particular the party responsible for the first stage of distribution on the national market;

(c) any other person, where necessary, with regard to cooperation in action taken to avoid risks arising from a product.

TITLE IV
Notification and Exchanges of Information

Article 7

1. Where a Member State takes measures which restrict the placing of a product or a product batch on the market or require its withdrawal from the market, such as provided for in Article 6 (1) (d) to (h), the Member State shall, to the extent that such notification is not required under any specific Community legislation, inform the Commission of the said measures, specifying its reasons for adopting them. This obligation shall not apply where the measures relate to an event which is local in effect and in any case limited to the territory of the Member State concerned.

2. The Commission shall enter into consultations with the parties concerned as quickly as possible. Where the Commission concludes, after such consultations, that the measure is justified, it shall immediately inform the Member State which initiated the action and the other Member States. Where the Commission concludes, after such consultations, that the measures is not justified, it shall immediately inform the Member State which initiated the action.

TITLE V
Emergency Situations and Action at Community Level

Article 8

1. Where a Member State adopts or decides to adopt emergency

measures to prevent, restrict or impose specific conditions on the possible marketing or use, within its own territory, of a product or product batch by reason of a serious and immediate risk presented by the said product or product batch to the health and safety of consumers, it shall forthwith inform the Commission thereof, unless provision is made for this obligation in procedures of a similar nature in the context of other Community instruments.

This obligation shall not apply if the effects of the risk do not, or cannot, go beyond the territory of the Member State concerned.

Without prejudice to the provisions of the first subparagraph, Member States may pass on to the Commission any information in their possession regarding the existence of a serious and immediate risk before deciding to adopt the measures in question.

2. On receiving this information, the Commission shall check to see whether it complies with the provisions of this Directive and shall forward it to the other Member States, which, in turn, shall immediately inform the Commission of any measures adopted.

3. Detailed procedures for the Community information system described in this Article are set out in the Annex. They shall be adapted by the Commission in accordance with the procedure laid down in Article 11.

Article 9

If the Commission becomes aware, through notification given by the Member States or through information provided by them, in particular under Article 7 or Article 8, of the existence of a serious and immediate risk from a product to the health and safety of consumers in various Member States and if:

(a) one or more Member States have adopted measures entailing restrictions on the marketing of the product or requiring its withdrawal from the market, such as those provided for in Article 6 (1) (d) to (h);

(b) Member States differ on the adoption of measures to deal with the risk in question;

(c) the risk cannot be dealt with, in view of the nature of the safety issue posed by the product and in a manner compatible with the urgency of the case, under the other procedures laid down by the specific Community legislation applicable to the product or category of products concerned; and

(d) the risk can be eliminated effectively only by adopting appropriate measures applicable at Community level, in order to ensure the protection of the health and safety of consumers and the proper functioning of the common market,

the Commission, after consulting the Member States and at the request of at least one of them, may adopt a decision, in accordance with the procedure laid down in Article 11, requiring Member States to take temporary measures from among those listed in Article 6 (1) (d) to (h).

Article 10

1. The Commission shall be assisted by a Committee on Product Safety Emergencies, hereinafter referred to as 'the Committee', composed of the representatives of the Member States and chaired by a representative of the Commission.

2. Without prejudice to Article 9 (c), there shall be close cooperation between the Committee referred to in paragraph 1 and the other Committees established by specific rules of Community law to assist the Commission as regards the health and safety aspects of the product concerned.

Article 11

1. The Commission representative shall submit to the Committee a draft of the measures to be taken. The Committee, having verified that the conditions listed in Article 9 are fulfilled, shall deliver its opinion on the draft within a time limit which the Chairman may lay down according to the urgency of the matter but which may not exceed one month. The opinion shall be delivered by the majority laid down in Article 148 (2) of the Treaty for adoption of decisions by the Council on a proposal from the Commission. The votes of the representatives of the Member States within the Committee shall be weighted in the manner set out in that Article. The Chairman shall not vote.

The Commission shall adopt the measures in question, if they are in accordance with the opinion of the Committee. If the measures proposed are not in accordance with the Committee's opinion, or in the absence of an opinion, the Commission shall forthwith submit to the Council a proposal regarding the measures to be taken. The Council shall act by a qualified majority.

If the Council has not acted within 15 days of the date on which the proposal was submitted to it, the measures proposed shall be adopted by the Commission unless the Council has decided against them by a simple majority.

2. Any measure adopted under this procedure shall be valid for no longer than three months. That period may be prolonged under the same procedure.

3. Member States shall take all necessary measures to implement the decisions adopted under this procedure within less than 10 days.

4. The competent authorities of the Member States responsible for carrying out measures adopted under this procedure shall, within one month, give the parties concerned an opportunity to submit their views and shall inform the Commission accordingly.

Article 12

The Member States and the Commission shall take the steps necessary to ensure that their officials and agents are required not to disclose information obtained for the purposes of this Directive which, by its nature, is covered by professional secrecy, except for information relating to the safety properties of a given product which must be made public if circumstances so require, in order to protect the health and safety of persons.

TITLE VI
Miscellaneous and final provisions

Article 13

This Directive shall be without prejudice to Directive 85/ 374 / EEC.

Article 14

1. Any decision adopted under this Directive and involving restrictions on the placing of a product on the market, or requiring its withdrawal from the market, must state the appropriate reasons on which it is based. It shall be notified as soon as possible to the party concerned and shall indicate the remedies available under the provisions in force in the Member State in question and the time

limits applying to such remedies.

The parties concerned shall, whenever feasible, be given an opportunity to submit their views before the adoption of the measure. If this has not been done in advance because of the urgency of the measures to be taken, such opportunity shall be given in due course after the measure has been implemented.

Measures requiring the withdrawal of a product from the market shall take into consideration the need to encourage distributors, users and consumers to contribute to the implementation of such measures.

2. Member States shall ensure that any measure taken by the competent authorities involving restrictions on the placing of a product on the market or requiring its withdrawal from the market can be challenged before the competent courts.

3. Any decision taken by virtue of this Directive and involving restrictions on the placing of a product on the market or requiring its withdrawal from the market shall be entirely without prejudice to assessment of the liability of the party concerned, in the light of the national criminal law applying in the case in question.

Article 15

Every two years following the date of adoption, the Commission shall submit a report on the implementation of this Directive to the European Parliament and the Council.

Article 16

Four years from the date referred to in Article 17 (1), on the basis of a Commission report on the experience acquired, together with appropriate proposals, the Council shall decide whether to adjust this Directive, in particular with a view to extending its scope as laid down in Article 1 (1) and Article 2 (a), and whether the provisions of Title V should be amended.

Article 17

1. Member States shall adopt the laws, regulations and administrative provisions necessary to comply with this Directive by 29 June 1994 at the latest. They shall forthwith inform the Commission thereof. The provisions adopted shall apply with effect from 29 June 1994.

2. When these measures are adopted by the Member States, they shall contain a reference to this Directive or be accompanied by such a reference on the occasion of their official publication. The methods of making such a reference shall be laid down by the Member States.

3. Member States shall communicate to the Commission the text of the provisions of national law which they adopt in the area covered by this Directive.

Article 18

Decision 89/45/EEC is hereby repealed on the date referred to in Article 17 (1).

Article 19

This Directive is addressed to the Member States.

Done at Luxembourg, 29 June 1992.

For the Council

The President

Carlos BORREGO

ANNEX

DETAILED PROCEDURES FOR THE APPLICATION OF THE COMMUNITY SYSTEM FOR THE RAPID EXCHANGE OF INFORMATION PROVIDED FOR IN ARTICLE 8

1. The system covers products placed on the market as defined in Article 2 (a) of this Directive.

Pharmaceuticals, which come under Directive 75/319/EEC and 81/851/EEC, and animals, to which Directive 82/894/EEC applies and products of animal origin, as far as they are covered by Directive 89/662/EEC, and the system for radiological emergencies which covers widespread contamination of products (Decision 87/ 600/Euratom), are excluded, since they are covered by equivalent notification procedures.

2. The system is essentially aimed at a rapid exchange of information in the event of a serious and immediate risk to the health and

safety of consumers. It is impossible to lay down specific criteria as to what, precisely, constitutes an immediate and serious risk; in this regard, the national authorities will therefore judge each individual case on its merits. It should be noted that, as Article 8 of this Directive relates to immediate threats posed by a product to consumers, products involving possible long-term risks, which call for a study of possible technical changes by means of directives or standards are not concerned.

3. As soon as a serious and immediate risk is detected, the national authority shall consult, insofar as possible and appropriate, the producer or distributor of the product concerned. Their point of view and the details which they supply may be useful both to the administrations of the Member States and to the Commission in determining what action should be taken to ensure that the consumer is protected with a minimum of commercial disruption. To these ends the Member States should endeavour to obtain the maximum of information on the products and the nature of the danger, without compromising the need for rapidity.

4. As soon as a Member State has detected a serious and immediate risk, the effects of which extend or could extend beyond its territory, and measures have been taken or decided on, it shall immediately inform the Commission. The Member State shall indicate that it is notifying the Commission under Article 8 of this Directive. All available details shall be given, in particular on:

(a) information to identify the product;

(b) the danger involved, including the results of any tests/analyses which are relevant to assessing the level of risk;

(c) the nature of the measures taken or decided on;

(d) information on supply chains where such information is possible.

Such information must be transmitted in writing, preferably by telex or fax, but may be preceded by a telephone call to the Commission. It should be remembered that the speed with which the information is communicated is crucial.

5. Without prejudice to point 4, Member States may, where appropriate, pass information to the Commission at the stage preceding the decision on the measures to be taken. Immediate contact, as soon as a risk is discovered or suspected, can in fact facilitate preventive action.

6. If the Member State considers certain information to be confidential, it should specify this and justify its request for confidentiality, bearing in mind that the need to take effective measures to protect consumers normally outweighs considerations of confidentiality. It should also be remembered that precautions are taken in all cases, both by the Commission and by the members of the network responsible in the various Member States, to avoid any unnecessary disclosure of information likely to harm the reputation of a product or series of products.

7. The Commission shall verify the conformity of the information received with Article 8 of this Directive, contact the notifying country, if necessary, and forward the information immediately by telex or fax to the relevant authorities in the other Member States with a copy to each permanent representation; these authorities may, at the same time as the transmission of the telex, be contacted by telephone. The Commission may also contact the Member State presumed to be the country or origin of the product to carry out the necessary verifications.

8. At the same time the Commission, when it considers it to be necessary, and in order to supplement the information received, can in exceptional circumstances institute an investigation of its own motion and/or convene the Committee on Emergencies provided for in Article 10 (1) of this Directive.

In the case of such an investigation Member States shall supply the Commission with the requested information to the best of their ability.

9. The other Member States are requested, wherever possible, to inform the Commission without delay of the following:

(a) whether the product has been marketed in its territory;

(b) supplementary information it has obtained on the danger involved, including the results of any tests/analyses carried out to assess the level of risk,

and in any case they must inform the Commission as soon as possible of the following:

(c) the measures taken or decided on, of the type mentioned in Article 8 (1) of this Directive;

(d) when the product mentioned in this information has been

found within their territory but no measures have been taken or decided on and the reasons why no measures are to be taken.

10. The Commission may, in the light of the evolution of a case and the information received from Member States under point 9 above, convene the above Committee on Emergencies in order to exchange views on the results obtained and to evaluate the measures taken. The Committee on Emergencies may also be convened at the request of a representative of a Member State.

11. The Commission shall, by means of its internal coordination procedures, endeavour to:

(a) avoid unnecessary duplication in dealing with notifications;

(b) make full use of the expertise available within the Commission;

(c) keep the other services concerned fully informed;

(d) ensure that discussions in the various relevant committees are held in accordance with Article 10 of this Directive.

12. When a Member State intends, apart from any specific measures taken because of serious and immediate risks, to modify its legislation by adopting technical specifications, the latter must be notified to the Commission at the draft stage, in accordance with Directive 83/189/EEC, if necessary, quoting the urgent reasons set out in Article 9 (3) of that Directive.

13. To allow it to have an overview of the situation, the Committee on Emergencies shall be periodically informed of all the notifications received and of the follow-up. With regard to points 8 and 10 above, and in those cases which fall within the scope of procedures and/or committees provided for by Community legislation governing specific products or product sectors, those committees shall be involved. In cases where the Committee on Emergencies is not involved and no provisions are made under 11 (d), the contact points shall be informed of any exchange of views within other committees.

14. At present there are two networks of contact points: the food products network and the non-food products network. The list of contact points and officials responsible for the networks with telephone, telex and fax numbers and addresses is confidential and

distributed to the members of the network only. This list enables contact to be established with the Commission and between Member States in order to facilitate clarification of points of detail. When such contacts between Member States give rise to new information of general interest, the Member States which initiated the bilateral contact shall inform the Commission. Only information received or confirmed through contact points in Member States may be considered as received through the rapid exchange of information procedure.

Every year the Commission shall carry out a review of the effectiveness of the network, of any necessary improvements and of the progress made in the communications technology between the authorities responsible for its operation.

ENDNOTES

1 OJ No C 156, 27. 6. 1990, p 8.

2 OJ No C 96, 17. 4. 1990, p. 283 and Decision of 11 June 1992 (not yet published in the Official Journal).

3 OJ No C 75, 26. 3. 1990, p. 1.

4 OJ No L 109, 26. 4. 1983, p. 8.

5 OJ No L 183, 14. 7. 1988, p. 34.

6 OJ No L 17, 21. 1. 1989, p. 51.

7 OJ No L 147, 9. 6. 1975, p. 13.

8 OJ No L 317, 6. 11. 1981, p. 1.

9 OJ No L 378, 31. 12. 1982, p. 58.

10 OJ No L 395, 30. 12. 1989, p. 13.

11 OJ No L 371, 30. 12. 1987, p. 76.

12 OJ No L 197, 18. 7. 1987, p. 33.

13 OJ No L 210, 7. 8. 1985, p. 29.

Appendix D — Japanese Law

Guide to the Product Liability Law (Law No. 85, 1994)

MITI—Ministry of International Trade and Industry

1. Introduction of the Product Liability System

Through the rapid development of science and technology and aggressive innovation in economic activities, Japan has attained a society of mass production and mass consumption. On the other hand, because consumers use and consume high-tech and complicated products daily, their safety primarily depends on product manufacturers.

Therefore, in order to change the principle of liability for damages in product-related accidents from "negligence" to "defect", and relieve the injured persons in a swift and appropriate manner, the Product Liability system, it is expected that the way of thinking and the approach concerning product safety of both the industry business segment and the consumer segment will change and improve.

2. What is Product Liability?

(1) Definition of Product Liability

Product Liability shall be defined as liability for damages in such case as follows:

a) in the case where due to a defect in the delivered product,

b) a life, a body or property of another person (including a third party not using or consuming the product directly, and a legal person as well as a natural person) is injured,

c) the person who manufactured, processed, imported or put his name, etc. on the product as business is liable for damages of the injured person.

(2) Significance of Introduction of the Product Liability Law

① Previously in Japan, claims for damages have usually been made based on the Civil Code Article No. 709 in case the injury is caused by a defect in the product. The Civil Code Article No. 709 employs the "fault-based liability (negligence) principle", and requires the "intention or fault" of the manufacturer, etc. as a condition for liability.

② The Product Liability Law takes the "defect in the product" as a condition for liability instead of the "intention or fault" of the manufacturer, etc. Therefore, after introduction of the Product Liability Law, the injured has only to verify the "defect in the product" for claiming damages.

The Difference of Liability Conditions between the Civil Code and the Product Liability Law

Civil Code Article No. 709	Product Liability Law (*)
1) The damage →	1) The damage
2) The intention or fault of the accused →	2) The defect in the product (at the time distribution commences)
3) The causal relationship between the damage and the intention or fault →	3) The causal relationship between the damage and the defect

*1 The Product Liability Law can be said to employ the "liability without fault principle", that is, the manufacturer, etc. is liable for damages if the injury is caused by a defect in the product regardless of whether it was his intention or fault. However, the manufacturer, etc. is not liable when there is no defect in the product.

*2 As the Product Liability Law is a means for claiming damages, the plaintiff side bears the burden of proof for the above-mentioned 1) -3).

③   The enactment of the Product Liability Law means a change in the liability rule from **fault-based liability principle to defect-based liability principle**

3. Points of the Product Liability Law

(1) Scope of the product

By definition, "product" means movable property manufactured or processed. Therefore, incorporeal property such as services, information, software, electricity, etc., and immovables are not the object of the Law.

Moreover, agricultural, forestal, marine and mineral products which are not processed artificially are not the object of the Law.

(2) Parties subject to liability

Parties subject to liability are as follows:

①   Manufacturer

②   Importer

③ Any person who puts his name, etc. on the product with such titles as "manufacturer" or "importer", or any person who puts his name, etc. on the product in a manner mistakable for its manufacturer or importer

(For instance, any person selling OEM products using his company brand name)

④ any person who, by putting his name, etc. on the product, may be recognized as its manufacturer-in-fact, in the light of a manner concerning manufacturing, processing, importation or sales, and other circumstances

(For instance, any person, even though he puts his name, etc. on the product with such titles as "seller" or "sales agency", who is socially recognized as its manufacturer-in-fact or is a sole distributor of the product)

(3) Concept of the term "defect"

A "defect" does not mean mere lack of quality of the product, but means lack of safety in the product which may cause the injury to life, body, or property.

In the law, the term "defect" is defined as "lack of safety that the product ordinarily should provide," taking into account "the nature of the product", "the ordinarily foreseeable manner of use of the product", "the time when the manufacturer, etc. delivered the product", and other circumstances concerning the product.

These three above-mentioned circumstances include such respective factors, as are presented below.

In the actual trial, while the weight of each factor is different depending on individual cases, these factors are comprehensively taken into account in judging whether the product is defective or not.

① Meaning of "the nature of the product"
This means the circumstances of the product itself, including factors such as the following:

   i)   representation of the product (instructions, warning, etc. to prevent accidents)

   ii) effectiveness and usefulness of the product (compared to its danger)

iii) cost vs. effect (the safety standard of products in the same price range)

iv) probability of occurrence of accident and its extent

v) ordinary use period and durable period of the product.

② Meaning of "the ordinarily foreseeable manner of use of the product".
This means the circumstances concerning use of the product, including factors such as the following:

vi) reasonably foreseeable use of the product

vii) possibility of preventing damage from occurring by the product user.

③ Meaning of "the time when the manufacturer, etc., delivered the product, including factors such as the following:

viii) situation at the time the product was delivered (the safety level required in society at the time the product was delivered)

ix) technological capabilities (the prior state of safety regulations and possibility of alternative design).

(4) Exemptions

① Development Risk Defense

The Product Liability Law admits 'Development Risk Defense" as an exemption. This means the manufacturer, etc. shall not be liable for damages, if the manufacturer, etc. proves that the state of "scientific or technical knowledge" at the time when the manufacturer, etc. delivered the product was not such as to enable the existence of the defect in the product to be discovered.

"Scientific or technical knowledge" means all the established knowledge that could influence the decision on the existence of the defect, and not the knowledge by a peculiar person but the total knowledge that objectively exists in society.

② Component or Raw Materiel Manufacturer's Defense

Insofar as components or raw materials are "products"—movable property manufactured or processed—their manufacturers are also subject to liability in the Law.

However, if the manufacturer, etc. of a component or raw material proves that the defect is substantially attributable to compliance with the instructions concerning the specifications given by the assembling manufacturer who incorporates the component of raw material into another product, and that the manufacturer, etc. is not negligent on occurrence of the defect, the manufacturer of the component or raw material shall not be liable for damages.

(5) Time Limitations

The right for damages provided in the Law shall be extinguished by prescription of the injured person or his legal representative does not exercise their rights within the following period:

A period of three years from the time when the injured person or his legal representative becomes aware of the damage and the liable party for the damage (short-term negative prescription).

A period of ten years from the time when the manufacturer, etc. delivered the product (long-term liable period).

Concerning introduction of the Product Liability Law, the cooperation of all divisions of a company are indispensable. Namely, not only development, design, manufacturing and quality control division, but also general affairs, law and consumer division, etc. are recommended to cooperate with each other on product safety measures.

In case injury to life, body, or property is caused by a defect in the product, all product-related manufacturers as well as the assembling manufacturer of the finished product shall be liable jointly and severally for the damages described in the Law.

Comparison of the Product Liability Law with the Product Liability system of the EU and US.

Applicable Laws

Japan: The Product Liability Law

EU: EC Product Liability Directive (Council Directive of 25 July 1985)

US: Judicial Precedents

Principle of Liability for Damages

Liability without Fault Principle (Defect-based Liability Principle).

Burden of Proof

The plaintiff side bears the burden of proof of damage, defect and causal relationship between defect and damage.

Adoption of Presumption Rule

Japan: No (flexible application of empirical rules and inference)

EU: No

US: No (Preponderance of the Evidence, Discovery)

Adoption of Development Risk Defense

Japan: Yes

EU: Yes (option: adopted by 12 of 14 countries)

US: Yes (state-of-the-art defense)

Liable Period

Japan: 10 years from the delivery of the product (10 years from the time the damage arises in case such damage as caused by accumulation of substances or others)

EU: 10 years from the delivery of the product

US: 10 years from the delivery of the product (in many states).

The Product Liability Law (Law No. 85, 1994)

(tentative translation)

Article 1 [Purpose]

The purpose of this Law is to relieve the injured person by setting forth liability of the manufacturer, etc. for damages when the injury on a life, a body, or property is caused by a defect in the product, and thereby to contribute to the stabilization and improvement of the people's life and to the sound development of the national economy.

Article 2 [Definitions]

(1) As used in this Law, the term "product" means movable property manufactured or processed.

(2) As used in this Law, the term "defect" means lack of safety that the product ordinarily should provide, taking into account the nature of the product, the ordinarily foreseeable manner of use of the product, the time when the manufacturer, etc. delivered the product, and other circumstances concerning the product.

(3) As used in this Law, the term "manufacturer, etc." means any one of the following:

    1. any person who manufactured, processed, or imported the product as business (hereinafter called just "manufacturer";

    2. any person who, by putting his name, trade name, trade mark or other feature (hereinafter call "representation of name, etc.") on the product presents himself as its manufacturer, or any person who puts the representation of name, etc. on the product in a manner mistakable for the manufacturer;

    3. apart from any person mentioned in the preceding subsec-

tions, any person who, by putting the representation of name, etc. on the product, may be recognized as its manufacturer-in-fact, in the light of manner concerning manufacturing, processing, importation or sales, and other circumstances.

Article 3 [Product Liability]

The manufacturer, etc. shall be liable for damages caused by the injury, when he injured someone's life, body or property by the defect in his delivered product which he manufactured, processed, imported or put the representation of name, etc. as described in subsection 2 or 3 of section 3 of Article 2 on. However, the manufacturer, etc. is not liable when only the defective product itself is damaged.

Article 4 [Exemptions]

In cases where Article 3 applies, the manufacturer, etc. shall not be liable as a result of Article 3 if he proves;

1. that the state of scientific or technical knowledge at the time when the manufacturer, etc. delivered the product was not such as to enable the existence of the defect in the product to be discovered; or

2. in the case where the product is used as a component or raw material of another product, that the defect is substantially attributable to compliance with the instruction concerning the specifications given by the manufacturer of the said another product, and that the manufacturer, etc. is not negligent on occurrence of the defect.

Article 5 [Time Limitations]

(1) The right for damages provided in Article 3 shall be extinguished by prescription if the injured person or his legal representative does not exercise such right within 3 years from the time when he becomes aware of the damage and the liable party for the damage. The same shall also apply upon the expiry of a period of 10 years from the time when the manufacturer, etc. delivered the product.

(2) The period in the latter sentence of section 1 of this Article shall be calculated from the time when the damage arises, where such damage is caused by the substances which are harmful to human health when they remain or accumulate in the body, or where the symptoms for such damage appear after a certain latent period.

Article 6 [Application of Civil Code]

In so far as this law does not provide otherwise, the liability of the manufacturer, etc. for damages caused by a defect in the product shall be subject to the provisions of the Civil Code (Law No. 89, 1896).

Supplementary Provisions

1. Enforcement Date, etc.
   This Law shall come into force the day after one year from the date of promulgation, and shall apply to the products delivered by the manufacturer, etc. after this Law comes into force.

2. Partial Amendment of the Law on Compensation for Nuclear Damage
   The Law on Compensation for Nuclear Damage (Law No. 147, 1961) shall be partially amended as follows:

In section 3 of Article 4 of that Law, "and the Law relating to the Limitation of the Liability of shipowners (Law No. 94, 1975) and the Product Liability Law (Law No. 85, 1994).

Consumer Affairs Division Industrial Policy Bureau

Ministry of International Trade and Industry

1-3-1, Kasumigaseki, Chiyoda-ku, Tokyo 100, Japan

Appendix E

Sources for More Information

The ISO 9000 series of standards is an evolving quality management system. Copies of standards are available for a fee from
ANSI, ASQ, ASTM and NSFI. To keep abreast of the latest
editions and be in a position to provide comment and input, it is
recommended that you join the US TAG. For more information
on membership to the US TAG, contact ASQ.

American Association for Laboratory Accreditation (A2LA)

656 Quince Orchard Road, #620
Gaithersburg, MD 20878-1409
Tel: 301-670-1377; Fax: 301-869-1495
Web: www.a2la.org

American National Standards Institute (ANSI)

11 West 42nd Street
New York, NY 10036
Tel: 212-642-4900; Fax: 212-398-0023
Web: www.ansi.org

American Society for Quality (ASQ)

611 East Wisconsin Avenue
Milwaukee, WI 53202-4606
Tel: 414-272-8575 or 800-248-1946
Fax: 414-272-1734
Web: www.asq.org

American Society for Testing and Materials (ASTM)

100 Bar Harbor Drive
West Conshohocken, PA 19428
Tel: 610-832-9500; Fax: 610-832-9555
Web: www.astm.org

Association for the Advancement of
Medical Instrumentation (AAMI)

3330 Washington Boulevard
Arlington, VA 22201-4598
Tel: 703-525-4890; Fax: 703-276-0793
Web: www.aami.org

Automotive Industry Action Group (AIAG)

Source of QS-9000
Dept. 77839, PO Box 77000
Detroit, MI 48277-0839
Tel: 248-358-3003; Fax: 248-358-3253
Web: www.aiag.org

Delegation of the Commission of the European Communities

3 Dag Hammarskjöld Plaza, 305 East 47th Street
New York, NY 10017-2301
Tel: 212-371-3804; Fax: 212-688-1013

International Forum for Management Systems (INFORM)

Publisher of…
THE INFORMED OUTLOOK — a twice-monthly newsletter on
management systems — and other books and training videos
15913 Edgewood Drive
Montclair, VA 22026
Tel: 703-680-1436; Fax: 703-680-1356
Web: www.INFORMINTL.COM

International Organization for Standardization (ISO)

Geneva, Switzerland
Tel: 011-41-22-749-0111
Fax: 011-41-22-733-3430
Web: www.iso.org

NSF International (NSFI)

PO Box 130140
Ann Arbor, MI 48113-0140
Tel: 313-769-8010; Fax: 313-769-0109

Registrar Accreditation Board (RAB)

611 East Wisconsin Avenue
Milwaukee, WI 53202-4606
Tel: 414-272-8575 or 800-248-1946
Fax: 414-272-1734

US Department of Commerce Office of Europe

Herbert C. Hoover Building, 14th and Constitution Avenue NW
Washington, DC 20230
Tel: 202-482-5276